I Can Learn from You

Boys as Relational Learners

MICHAEL REICHERT

AND

RICHARD HAWLEY

Harvard Education Press

Cambridge, Massachusetts

Youth Development
and Education Series

Library of Congress Control Number 2013951066

Paperback ISBN 978-1-61250-664-7
Library Edition ISBN 978-1-61250-665-4

Published by Harvard Education Press,
an imprint of the Harvard Education Publishing Group

Harvard Education Press
8 Story Street
Cambridge, MA 02138

Cover Design: Ciano Design
Cover Photo: MachineHeadz/E+/Getty Images

The typefaces used in this book are Sabon and Ocean Sans

CONTENTS

INTRODUCTION

WE ARE SITTING AROUND a conference table with a group of older boys enrolled in a school in Toronto. We are discussing when and how they respond positively to a teacher.

Three of the boys, unalike physically or in their mannerisms, begin talking animatedly about their economics teacher who, one of them claims, "ignited" him. The boys speak of this man with something like reverence. They describe the atmosphere of his classroom as somehow charged with importance. "It's a class," one of them says, "where you wouldn't *think* of acting out." The teacher's presence, they explain, is not strict or commanding. The elevated seriousness of his class seems to stem from the teacher's own seriousness about his subject—the boys speak of his "passion"—and the care he takes in responding to what they say and the written work they hand in. "There is just something about him," one of the boys says. "You would be ashamed not to do your work, your best work."

Across the city we are talking to a similar group of boys enrolled in another school. The discussion has turned to teachers the boys felt they could not respond to. One boy's face hardened noticeably when he described a hurtful encounter with a history teacher. The boy, self-described as frequently in trouble, had been sent out of class for a dress code violation: wearing a colored T-shirt under his code-required dress shirt. Since his outer shirt was in code and (he felt) the undershirt didn't really show, he was angry at being called out. As he stormed out into the hall, the teacher followed him and continued to berate him, concluding with "you are such a *punk*." And what was your response to that, we asked. The boy said with conviction, "I *hate* him." But, we persisted, you are still in the class; you have to work for him, right? The boy said, "I'm not doing *anything* in that class. He can flunk me, they can kick me out—I'm not doing anything."

In the course of a daylong workshop with students and teachers at a school in the United Kingdom, a seventeen-year-old boy recounted a French class in which he underperformed, did not care for his teacher, and was well aware that his teacher did not care for him. The boy reported disengaging from the class, handing in partially prepared, sloppy work, which his teacher duly awarded the failing marks it merited. By year's end what had begun as wariness on the part of boy and teacher had devolved into mutual resentment and dislike. In the course of exchanges between the boy telling the story and the roomful of teachers who heard it, one teacher—a teacher of French—asked the boy, with some feeling, whether he didn't feel a responsibility to do what he could to repair the relationship himself. The boy paused to reflect. Then he said, "I suppose so. I can see that I was not easy to teach or to deal with—but I was *thirteen*."

Some boys thrive in school; many do not. At present there is a growing consensus worldwide not only that boys' scholastic performance is failing to keep up with a rapidly evolving knowledge economy, but also that boys and young men more generally are failing to find productive places in the work force and community. However troubling such claims about boys' scholastic and other prospects may be generally, boys' school troubles and other failures to achieve are neither universal nor normative.

The intriguing fact of the matter is that some boys in some schools—in fact, some boys in most schools—find their footing, become productively engaged, and even exceed expectations.

Moreover, on the evidence of two international studies, we have found that many of these boys succeed dramatically, regardless of their tested ability level, ethnic or economic status, the type of school they attend, or the region in which they live. We undertook this research to determine how and why certain boys succeed and, more specifically, how the quality of their relationships to their teachers contributed to their success.

Recognizing the promise of the accumulated findings pointing to the positive effect of relationship in the improvement of scholastic achievement generally—and for school-resistant boys in particular—our Relational Teaching study attempted to locate the specific relational strategies teachers and boys identified in successful learning partnerships. The common patterns and features we discovered in those relationships varied little with school type, school culture, scholastic discipline, or with the age, length of tenure, or gender of the teacher.

In the following chapters we document how boys and their teachers assess productive and unproductive relationships with one another. Drawing on both their written and oral narratives, we identify the elements composing effective *working alliances* between teachers and their students, including the necessary gestures teachers must extend in their unique role as *relationship manager*. In addition to conveying to their students mastery of their subjects and a clear, humane set of behavioral expectations, relationally effective teachers are characterized by: (1) reaching out, often beyond standard classroom protocols, to locate and meet particular student needs, (2) locating and responding to student's individual interests and talents, (3) sharing common interests and talents, (4) sharing common characteristics, such as ethnicity, faith, and learning approaches, (5) being willing, when appropriate, to disclose personal experiences, (6) being willing to accommodate a measure of opposition, and (7) being willing to reveal some degree of personal vulnerability. In contrast with these generous and thoughtful examples of successful strategies, stories of relational breakdown—also common—revealed more stressed and defensive teachers whose concerns with self-management obscured their responsibility as relational manager.

A PROBLEM AND A REMEDY

In this study we both address the causes of contemporary boys' scholastic decline and offer a means to reverse it. Again, some boys—in schools of all kinds all over the world—are thriving today. Scholastically struggling, chronically underachieving boys are finding their feet, becoming engaged in school challenges, and mastering required material. Scholastically capable boys are deepening their engagement in their required fields of study and are exceeding teachers' expectations and their own.

Our previous study of effective teaching strategies with boys and this relational study suggest that boys are not only relationally receptive, but they may be *especially* relationally receptive—indeed, unlikely to thrive scholastically outside of caring, supportive relationships with their teachers.

We will show that boys of all types thrive in school when they are engaged by teachers who build and maintain those connections through specific relational gestures that invite boys' trust and effort. Moreover, teachers of all types and in all disciplines are capable of acquiring and practicing these effective gestures. From teachers' own stories, corroborated by those of boys, we believe that relationally ineffective teachers can become effective, and relationally effective teachers can become more so.

To reverse the worrying educational trajectory of boys generally, we must reexamine historic assumptions that boys are nonempathic, relationally insensitive, and somehow school-averse. Boys—*some* boys—are clearly, observably not that way. And as our research has indicated, boys who appear to be that way are transformed when they are relationally engaged.

A promising first step in improving the relational climate in schools is to dispel prevailing stereotypes of developing boys as alienated, unconnected, and unconnectable beings. Relationally effective teachers demonstrate how to engage resistant boys. The boys so engaged are generous in their praise of and gratitude to their teachers. The teachers who succeed in forging such relationships count those experiences as the principal reason they continue their work.

CHAPTER ONE

■ ■ ■

Listening to Boys
and Their Teachers

EFFECTIVE TEACHING—including the effective teaching of boys—takes place every day and is easily identified. In 2008–2009, we conducted a study of successful teaching practices in schools in six countries—the United States, Canada, the United Kingdom, Australia, New Zealand, and South Africa—that was commissioned by the International Boys' Schools Coalition (www.theibsc.org). Though the single-sex schools in our sample represent a special school context, their particular focus was compatible with our desire to investigate teaching practices reported to work with boys (see the appendix). Moreover, it soon became clear that our findings in single-sex contexts were helpfully applicable to other kinds of schools, including coeducational ones.

From the schools that participated in our Teaching Boys study, we solicited middle- and upper-school teachers' and seventh-through twelfth-grade boys' online responses to a basic prompt.

The participating teachers responded to the following prompt: "Please describe an effective practice you have employed. Tell the story of the practice, as if you are explaining it to a colleague in another subject, or perhaps to a younger teacher who is looking for guidance."

We were aware that teachers' narrative gifts would likely vary a great deal, and we knew that the depth and clarity of their narrated "effective practice" would vary accordingly. In sum, we did not know what kind of quality and substance we would get from busy teachers asked to engage in yet another task imposed on them. As it happened, most teachers in the participating schools responded with considerable care and detail. The practices teachers submitted were not merely effective but were, for many, what they considered their best lessons. We received nearly a thousand teacher narratives in all, representing a majority of each school's faculty working with adolescent boys.

After a preliminary review of the submissions, we sorted responses into a number of thematic categories that emerged from the various lessons described. The convergence of similar practice—across disciplines, length of tenure, school region and culture—was pronounced. While we summarized lessons under thematic headings based upon their dominant element, nearly every reported lesson included multiple elements—as when a teacher devised a *game* wherein *teams* of boys created a *product* that would be judged *competitively*.

Unsure as we were about how thoroughly and thoughtfully the surveyed teachers would address the task, we were even more concerned whether boys, under conditions of promised anonymity, would respond seriously to their prompt: "Tell us the story of a classroom experience that stands out as being especially memorable for you."

We received responses from nearly fifteen hundred students, spanning ages twelve to nineteen and representing considerable ethnic and economic diversity as well as a wide range of scholastic motivation and achievement. Despite our injunction against naming names, many respondents ignored this prompt and proceeded, often with great feeling, to relate their appreciation of particular teachers: their patience, their impressive mastery of their subject, their willingness to offer extra help, and, strikingly often, their sense of humor. This Canadian tenth grader's tribute is a representative example:

> This took place in Computer Studies in grade ten. When we began programming, I had difficulty understanding how it worked and how to do it. However, the teacher was very understanding toward me and helped me through the whole way. She never gave up on me even though I kept on having difficulty, and finally, after many morning and lunch extra help sessions, a light finally turned on in my mind and I understood everything. I was able to get a really good score on the big test of that unit, but that is not the point of the story. The thing that is memorable is that she never gave up on me and always believed that I could do it. There is no way that I could've understood this confusing and complex unit without her extensive aid. She went the extra mile to help me, and that's what makes this school so great.

THREE GENERAL FINDINGS

In addition to helping us to categorize the types of lessons found to be especially effective with boys, the student and teacher narratives from our Teaching Boys study revealed three overarching findings. The first was that boys tend to elicit the kind of pedagogy they need. Many of the teachers and boys described how some current practice was visibly not working. Boys were disengaged, inattentive, and even obstructive in response. The unsatisfactory student feedback stimulated teachers to adjust their material, delivery, and classroom setting until the boys' responses improved.

In teachers' narratives, there was no sense of wise and all-knowing practitioners applying time-honored and proven techniques. To the contrary, many teachers acknowledged prior frustration and even outright failure in the process of coming to their favored practice. Teaching more often involves a kind of feedback dynamic by which ineffective practice disengages boys, prompting teachers to adjust pedagogy until responsiveness and performance improve. Lessons identified as effective had been "chafed" into being through sustained interactions between teachers and boys. These instructional successes resulted not so much from teachers always getting their pedagogy right but more from their ability to sustain relationship while they figured things out.

The second finding was that successful lessons often introduced an element—an inspired novelty, kinetic activity, the adrenal boost of a game or a dramatic opportunity to assume a role—that was transitive to, or carried, the intended learning outcome. These transitive elements, often not directly associated with the lesson at hand, serve to arouse and hold student attention and interest. In other words, the motor activity or the adrenal boost of competing or the power of an unexpected surprise in the classroom serves not merely to engage or delight; it is transitive to—it attaches to and carries along—a specific lesson.

For example, in a British teacher's narrative of teaching *Romeo and Juliet* to his early adolescent boys, he introduces the discipline of stage swordplay. As the boys train, practice, and master some of the conventions of swordsmanship, they are engaged in a number of ways: the training is physically rigorous; it is dramatic, holding even the faint promise of danger;and it is novel. But, as the teacher's account reveals, it is also transitive to a deeper, more enlivened reading of those scenes in which Tybalt slays Mercutio and Romeo slays Tybalt—and to the play as a whole. The active exertions infuse the experience of tackling a dense, rich text with an altogether different kind of energy, appreciation, and attention.

The third major finding of the Teaching Boys study came to us almost exclusively from the students' responses. It surprised and, for a time, puzzled us. We had asked boys and teachers simply to narrate a lesson. But while the teachers adhered strictly to the prompt and wrote about a specific project or lesson, boys seemed unable to do this. They not only mentioned teachers' names, they also wrote about them with great feeling. At length it dawned on us:

the boys were unable to discuss effective lessons without describing the teacher conveying it. "Boys," we concluded, "experience their teachers before they experience the lessons they teach."[1]

The overall substance and tone of the student responses—including their refusal, if not their inability, to refrain from naming and relating instances of valued personal connections with their teachers—strongly suggested that the establishment of an affective connection is a precondition for the successful conveyance of scholastic material. This conclusion is supported by the work of Miriam Raider-Roth, professor of education at University of Cincinnati, who proposed the "relational learner" as the most apt model for how students acquire knowledge: "Just as the theory of the relational self postulates that the self is born and develops in the cradle and life of relationships, so the notion of the relational learner postulates that the learning self is constructed and developed within the relationships of school."[2]

The fact that boys' accounts of successful lessons tended to be relational, while their teachers focused almost exclusively on the substance of their lessons and on elements of their pedagogy, led us to a clearer understanding of how and why boys engage in and disengage from classroom instruction. The boys described no single "type" of effective teacher. Some shared stories of being uplifted by their teacher's humor, passion, and care; others related their positive responses to highly structured, demanding, "no nonsense" teachers, especially when they found those teachers to be "fair" and personally interested in them. In sum, the boys in our Teaching Boys study indicated their willingness to engage in classroom work, to suspend prior resistance—to *try*—for teachers to whom they were able to relate.

THE RELATIONAL TEACHING STUDY

While our Teaching Boys study enabled us to identify and to some extent document the importance of relationship in effective teaching, we did not specifically investigate how teachers conceptualize or construct the relational aspect of their pedagogy. What was for us the surprising centrality of relationship in boys' accounts of successful teaching was largely unacknowledged in the teacher narratives, which focused almost exclusively on the substance and delivery of their lessons. We realized we needed to understand better how both boys and teachers approached relationship in classroom settings and, if possible, identify the particular understandings, dispositions, and skills that promoted productive relationships, as well as those that prevented them or caused them to break down. If we were able to do this, we believed we would be able to heighten practicing teachers' awareness of relationship's place in boys' scholastic progress, help teachers become more intentional in their approach to relationships, and offer useful examples and strategies for effective relationship formation.

As we presented our Teaching Boys study to various school faculties, it was clear that the relational finding resonated strongly with teachers, although they found it difficult to articulate their own relational practices. Some drew upon general notions like "emotional intelligence" to describe what they meant, but the boys' narratives in our Teaching Boys study indicated that many factors other than their teachers' emotional awareness bore on their willingness to enter into productive relationships.

To better understand the part relationship played in boys' scholastic success, we sought to design a research study that would reveal relational dynamics at work across a wide range of schools, teachers, countries, and cultures. To detail the features of their successes and the conditions facilitating them, this study would once again require soliciting narrative accounts from both boys and teachers. Given the affective and not easily quantifiable elements of relationships, we also wanted to refine and deepen our understanding of the relationship narratives through a series of intimate focus groups with boys and teachers, as well as a number of workshops in which boys and teachers responded to our preliminary findings.

The Relational Teaching project was able to move forward because, once again, the International Boys' Schools Coalition commissioned a research team from the Center for the Study of Boys' and Girls' Lives (www.csbgl.org) to undertake the work. Of particular concern in this second study was to shed light on the relational conditions that enable boys from more stressed and marginalized groups to succeed in school. Accordingly we doubled our school sample and included urban and fully state-supported schools that serve significant numbers of minority, immigrant, and economically struggling families.

Like the Teaching Boys study, the Relational Teaching study followed the model of action research, which consists of two parts: (1) a collaborative "diagnosis" of the target social situation, and (2) an intervention in which positive, stakeholder-driven change is developed and tested.[3]

The Relational Teaching project thus sought to address these research questions:

- Can we describe the relational dimension in teachers' pedagogy, mapping the skills and processes involved?
- Can individual teachers be helped to reflect upon and improve these relational teaching skills?
- Can schools create professional learning contexts to help teachers sharpen these relational skills?

An online survey solicited narratives from over eleven hundred teachers in thirty-six schools of different sorts, asking how they achieved satisfying and scholastically productive relationships with boys—as well as how they experienced barriers that they were unable to overcome. In the same manner we surveyed nearly fourteen hundred adolescent boys from the same schools about their positive and negative relationships with their teachers. Once survey responses were collected from participating schools, the research team proceeded to analyze our data, organizing the narrative responses of both teachers and boys into defining categories.

These preliminary findings were then shared with teachers and students in a series of focus groups and multischool conferences, allowing us to elicit further feedback. We conducted focus groups, workshops, and conference calls with teams of teachers, staff, and students in each of the six countries from which schools were recruited.

The thousands of pages of survey narratives, recorded interviews, and field notes from the workshops composed a daunting volume of data, which nevertheless revealed a number of clear findings: patterns of relational practice that held true across national boundaries, teaching disciplines, teacher gender, student ability level, and school type or size. Throughout the project period, but especially in the course of group discussions and live interviews, we were impressed by participants' candor and willingness to disclose both positive and negative relational experiences. In so responding, both boys and teachers made it clear to us that relationship *mattered* to them—and was indeed the very heart of their common endeavor.

CHAPTER TWO

■ ■ ■

Boys' Underperformance
in School

OVER THE PAST FEW YEARS a provocative thesis about the future of Western societies has been proposed: that we might be reaching the "end of men." One version of this thesis asks whether, given demographic and economic trends, "women are not just catching up anymore; they are becoming the standard by which success is measured." This point of view celebrates women's progress and reflects a current zeitgeist that notes the uncertain position of men within a new gender order. As writer David Brooks opined in a recent column, "Over the past few decades millions of men have been caught on the wrong side of a historic transition, unable to cross the threshold into the new economy." In the scholastic realm demographers have predicted a steady decline in male performance such that by the year 2050, "women will outrank men academically in most parts of the world."[1]

There is little question that a scholastic achievement gap exists between boys and girls, but there is considerable debate about how the gap should be understood and, in particular, whether it represents something new. The notion that growing boys and formal schooling are a problematic match was culturally well established by the sixteenth century. In Shakespeare's *Romeo and Juliet*, Romeo compares his reluctance to leave Juliet's side to a schoolboy's reluctance to study: "Love goes from love as a schoolboy to his books." Jaques's famous "All the world's a stage" soliloquy in *As You Like It* portrays the schoolboy condition as one of the eternal, if grim, stages of the male life cycle: "the whining schoolboy with his satchel and shining morning face creeping to school."

Michele Cohen, an educational historian, points out that concern about boys' scholastic underachievement was noted by John Locke in the late seventeenth century, supporting a possibility that, when compared to girls, "boys have always underachieved." Moreover, she maintains, boys' underachievement has "never been seriously addressed." Also from the academy, Marcus Weaver-Hightower points out that there have been concerns about boys' reading achievement since at least the 1930s.[2]

Complicating matters is the significant educational progress exhibited by girls in countries that have embraced gender equity reforms. Analyses show that a country's scores on measures of gender equality correlate positively with girls' achievement, reducing or eliminating the math/science gap historically favoring boys while increasing the reading gap favoring girls. Some theorists have suggested that the extension of educational opportunity to girls and their resulting progress has given rise to a "moral panic" about boys' educational struggles, mobilizing cultural and political movements to "recuperate" dominant forms of masculinity.[3]

Perhaps motivated by such panic, "boy friendly" policies have been adopted at both local and national levels. A report by the Commonwealth Secretariat, *Boys' Underachievement in Education*, suggests the degree to which southern hemisphere countries have intensified their focus on boys. In Australia, the parliamentary-level report *Boys: Getting It Right* and the subsequent *Boys' Education Lighthouse Schools* policy sought to address the gender achievement gap by drawing from popular (though unproven) theories of essential differences between boys' and girls' learning styles. As gender concerns in general have been translated into policy worldwide, girls' scholastic gains have brought boys' educational standing into sharper relief.[4]

How significant is the actual gap in boys' and girls' scholastic achievement? The Program for International Student Assessment (PISA) coordinated by the Organization for Economic Cooperation and Development (OECD) has measured the school performance of fifteen-year-olds in over sixty countries every three years since 2000; the 2009 results, emphasizing reading literacy, were released in December 2010. Those results showed gender differences in reading favoring girls in all countries and in all educational systems, ranging from 9 points in Columbia to 62 points in Albania. The National Assessment of Educational Progress (NAEP) in the United States has corroborated these PISA trends, with boys trailing girls in literacy outcomes since the test was first administered. In the 2007 test, boys were 7 points behind girls by fourth grade and 10 points by eighth.[5]

Thomas Mortensen of the Pell Institute for the Study of Opportunity in Higher Education has been sounding alarms about the diverging social and scholastic trajectories of boys and girls for over a decade. His 2006 study, *The Changing World of Work for Men (and Women)*, charted rising trends in women's employment, education, leadership, and civic participation while noting the declining trends in men's employment, income, education, measures of well-being, and civic participation. In a 2011 study, *Economic Change Effects on Men and Implications for the Education of Boys*, he documented further declines in men's college enrollment, labor force participation, mean wages, and increases in unemployment, incarceration, poverty, and suicide.[6]

The troubling scholastic trajectory of males is particularly pronounced at the university level and beyond. International studies, such as those conducted by the United Kingdom's Higher Education Policy Institute (www.hepi.ac.uk) concluded an analysis of education and employment outcomes with a highly cautionary projection: "In our view of even greater concern is the possibility that current trends take us to a situation where higher education and the related professions are overwhelmingly female, and where the only men to progress to higher education are those from the most advantaged socio-economic groups."[7]

Some commentators on these trends argue that gender differences determine educational achievement less dramatically than differences of race or socioeconomic condition. Sara Mead drafted a widely distributed report for the think tank *Education Sector* that argued, "There's no doubt that some groups of boys—particularly Hispanic and black boys and boys from low-income homes—are in real trouble. But the predominant issues for them are race and class, not gender." In fact, some have seen the focus on boys' education as a ploy to distract attention and resources from efforts to correct class and race inequities and argue that this approach has been particularly effective in the United States. As Weaver-Hightower wrote, "Conservative movements of all types have rallied around boys' education, and here [in the United States] they have been more successful in turning back progressive gains and reestablishing the hegemony of males and patriarchy than anywhere else."

But while racial marginalization and poverty undeniably bear negatively on scholastic achievement, it is important to note that within each racial and class group, masculine norms compound or "inflect" these effects—to the extent that boys stand at the very bottom of achievement rankings for all groups of color. Whatever the relative causal impact on boys' scholastic progress posed by race, class, or gender, it is critical to understand, as Pedro Noguera of New York University has proposed, "the ways in which boys respond and adapt to their social and cultural environment." Few would argue that masculine norms shape the opportunities and constraints of boyhood in ways that intersect with these other social forces.[8]

A wide variety of pundits and social theorists continue to hold forth on boys' educational performance, not always helpfully. Some point out that boy "panics" have occurred routinely whenever contemporary expressions of masculinity come under fire. Others argue that the present preoccupation with boys' educational achievement is linked to the pressures of the global knowledge-based economy and a growing culture of individual consumerism. Still others suggest that the cultural "detraditionalization" of gender roles deepens these broader social and economic changes. Debbie Epstein and colleagues have identified three misleading characterizations of boys' education that have become prominent in popular media: "poor boys," "failing schools," and "boys will be boys" discourses. Arguments maintaining that successful efforts to better engage and instruct girls have somehow "feminized schools," thus contributing to male disengagement, have been challenged by evidence showing that advances in equality have positively affected all children and have improved school climates in general.[9]

Statistical "gaps" and dire demographic forecasts aside, we maintain that there need be no "end of men" on the horizon. As the scholastic gains of girls and women have shown, with humane advocacy and a commitment to a clearer understanding of the obstacles, children of either gender can improve their scholastic performance. Educators are largely in agreement that "a more sophisticated approach to boys' education" is called for—one that, among other points, addresses the conditions of boys' lives that normalize and thus contribute to the scholastic struggles of boys *in general*. Contrary to the characterizations of boys and young men commonly conveyed in the popular culture, those participating in our study—from diverse economic and racial conditions—did not find their schooling aversive. In fact, we found no evidence for anything like an inherent resistance to learning on the part of males. As one British sociologist and gender theorist put it: "Men's resistance to change is not reducible to their psychic obstinacy or incapacity. Men can and do change. Resistance to change is also bound up with the persisting gender routines which characterize most of the wider economic, social, and political structures of contemporary society."[10]

Central to these persisting routines is the meaning of *boyhood*. In the inaugural issue of a new scholarly publication, *Thymos: Journal of Boyhood Studies*, the editors invited readers to consider "a phenomenon that is by no means intuitively obvious": the boy. The very purpose of the new field of Boyhood Studies is to sort through myth and culture for a more grounded understanding of male development. The term *boyhood* itself, the editors proposed, is a relatively recent acknowledgment of the particular status of younger males, first seriously explored in the eighteenth-century writings of Jonathan Swift. How boys are understood and regarded, how they are positioned and treated within the institutional contexts of boyhood, must inform contemporary debates about their vitality.[11]

An eruption of literature exploring contemporary notions of boyhood appeared at the end of the twentieth century as journalists and scholars wrestled with the prevailing myths, norms, and assumptions bearing on boys' personal and school lives. In *Raising Cain*, Dan Kindlon and Michael Thompson discussed "destructive boy archetypes" that operate unconsciously on parents and teachers to skew their perceptions in ways that confound efforts to meet boys' actual needs. In a similar vein, William Pollack, author of another best-selling book, *Real Boys: Rescuing Our Sons from the Myths of Boyhood*, attributed boys' unsatisfying and often inappropriate socialization to their being compressed into an unproductive range of attitudes and behavior due to a culturally imposed "boy code." Michael Kimmel extrapolated these insights to college-age males in his findings about *Guyland*.[12]

While many writers and thinkers inside and outside the academic world have endeavored to describe boys' overall condition, too few have grounded their analyses in systematic observations of boys themselves. Both of our recent studies, Teaching Boys and Relational Teaching, have sought to fill this observational void by asking large, international samples of boys and their teachers about their mutual experience: what works and what does not in their shared scholastic enterprise.

Again, the prominent *relational* finding from our initial study puzzled us at first. The overall substance and tone of the student responses—including boys' refusal, if not their inability, to refrain from naming and relating instances of valued personal connections—strongly suggested that the establishment of an affective connection is a necessary condition for the successful conveyance of scholastic material. Especially for boys facing difficult social stresses or who were scholastically struggling, the issue was not what subject matter or instructional approach would engage their attention and elicit their effort, but *for whom* they would do those things.

Boys' responsiveness to the relational dimension of their school work seemed to us unremarked and underexplored in research addressing boys' school performance, although there has been some recent attention paid to their relational expectations and needs generally. In her twenty-year international study of boys' personal friendships, Niobe Way discovered a depth of mutual regard and interdependency among those she studied that led her to conclude that "a false story" about boys has dominated the popular mind: "My studies furthermore reveal a disconnection between the cultural construction of boyhood and boys' lived experiences. The general lack of interest in the scholarly and popular culture regarding the dynamics of close friendships among males, combined with boys' passion for these relationships, their emotional acuity, and the significance they give them, suggests that our expectations and stereotypes of boys are preventing us from seeing boys—their social and emotional desires and capacities—in broad daylight."[13]

The touching and unguarded expression of relational needs by boys persuaded Way to challenge the prevailing stereotypes representing them as nonrelational, or at least less relational than girls. Her report of boys' views on their relationships with friends parallels our own regarding boys' views of their teachers. Finding a profound contrast between boys' actual extension and reception of empathy and cultural myths portraying boys as individualistic and relationally numb, Way recommends that families, communities, and schools support boys' resistance to these cultural distortions of masculinity. From our research on boys in school, we find little support for conventional portrayals of boys as "too cool for school."

The link between the quality of teacher-student relationships and academic achievement has become a focal point for recent research. This is due in part to the fact that research attempting to link *nonrelational* instructional variables to student performance has tended to come up dry. A major summary of teacher effectiveness studies commissioned for the National Comprehensive Center for Teacher Quality concluded that "research has not been very successful at identifying the specific teacher qualifications, characteristics, and classroom practices that are most likely to improve student learning." Studies linking student performance to discrete, quantifiable teacher variables such as teachers' academic qualifications or personal characteristics found that "unobserved" and "intangible" variables accounted for the majority of variation in student achievement attributable to instructional factors.[14]

One of those intangible factors, the quality of the teacher-student relationship, is beginning to be better understood. Key research in the United States has described teacher-student relationships as the "developmental infrastructure" upon which a child's school experience is built. From their assessment of the state-mandated policies to make Australian schools more "boy friendly," Bob Lingard, Wayne Martino, and Martin Mills concluded, "It will be pedagogy, not the color of classroom walls, male teachers, the brightness of light bulbs, or single-sex classes, that will improve the academic outcomes of those boys who are currently disengaged from schooling."[15]

Over the last decade, a number of large-scale studies also pointed to the importance of student-teacher relationships. PISA recently cited "positive student-teacher relationships" to explain the progress made by students from the participating nations. In 2009 testing, it found that 85 percent of students across all of the participating countries got along well with their teachers, 67 percent reported that their teachers "really listen," and 66 percent reported that their teachers were "interested in their well-being." Yet, the PISA study also found considerable variation in countries' index of student-teacher relations, ranging from 80 percent positive assessments to as low as 28 percent.[16]

In the United States, the Gates Foundation launched the Measuring Effective Teaching (MET) project in 2009 to "test new approaches to recognizing effective teaching." Working in seven urban U.S. school districts with three thousand teachers who agreed to have their lessons videotaped and analyzed, the MET project collected a great deal of test and survey data. In a report on early findings, the research team wrote, "the average student knows effective teaching when he or she experiences it." The MET project utilized the Tripod surveys, which sample the "7 Cs" of effective teaching (care, control, clarify, challenge, captivate, confer, consolidate). Though concerned primarily with evaluation systems, the MET project lends additional support to two central conclusions from our study: that students hold effective teaching as a core value in their relationships with teachers and that the relational dimension is one of several that define teacher quality.[17]

In New Zealand, John Hattie determined that teacher "quality"—as perceived by students—is the most powerful factor explaining student achievement and that the warmth of teacher-student relations was a central factor in that perceived quality. In Australia, Andrew Martin has called attention to the relational dimension in his many studies of student motivation. In recent work, he has advocated specifically for "connective instruction," an approach that integrates personal relationship with subject content and pedagogy.[18]

Stepping back from the perspective of educational research, it is hardly surprising that relational dynamics should play a critical role in scholastic engagement and achievement. Scholars in the field of psychological attachment have long held that children enjoying secure attachment relationships thrive in meeting developmental challenges generally, including scholastic challenges. Even more promising is the finding of researchers that the negative effects of prior insecure attachments can be corrected by subsequent secure ones—with corresponding scholastic and other gains. As one research team concluded, "if teachers are able to behave in ways that *disconfirm* the insecure child's internal working models, then a secure relationship can develop between teacher and child."[19]

The evidence further suggests that positive learning relationships may be especially beneficial in reaching children at the bottom of the achievement gap. Of particular concern are the 30–50 percent of students who come to school with insecure attachment histories and who, because of resistant behaviors, are harder for teachers to deal with. In a recent analysis of nearly one hundred studies linking teaching relationships with student engagement and student achievement, a Dutch research team found that both positive and negative teacher-student relationships affected scholastic achievement from mild to significant degrees. Stronger positive effects were found with older students, stronger negative effects with younger students.[20]

A new model offered by researchers in the emotional intelligence tradition relates classroom emotional climate—the quality of social and emotional interactions among and between students and teachers—to student engagement and academic achievement. Following an experimental test of their model, the research team concluded, "We have shown that when a classroom climate is characterized by warm, respectful, and emotionally supportive relationships, students perform better academically in part because they are more emotionally engaged in the learning process."[21]

However consistently these psychological and developmental findings confirm that the depth and quality of teacher-student relationships are scholastically consequential, merely recognizing the phenomenon does not in itself transform relational practice. Not just educational and psychological research, but also a rich succession of fiction, memoir, and film, has attested to the transformative effects of positive, caring mentors—and to the awfulness of cold, mean-spirited ones—and yet the relational dimension has remained unremarked and undertheorized. A consortium of writers and researchers convened in 2004 to discuss relational pedagogy. The group subsequently composed a *Manifesto of Relational Pedagogy*, which cautioned: "A fog of forgetfulness is looming over education. Forgotten in the fog is that education is about human beings. And as schools are places where human beings get together, we have also forgotten that education is primarily about human beings who are in relation with one another."[22]

Befogged or not, the actual components of relational teaching have been elusive, even as they have long been implicitly recognized as central. In a 1914 autobiographical essay, *Some Reflections on Schoolboy Psychology*, Sigmund Freud recalled that he and his classmates "were from the first equally inclined to love and hate our teachers, to criticize and respect them." The assumption that any given school will inevitably be staffed by both relationally deft and relationally deaf adults has long gone unchallenged, due in part to educational thinkers' willingness to see an inevitable, insoluble conflict between the necessities of schooling and the developmental needs of children. But *is* the conflict inevitable and insoluble? Is there a good reason to believe that individual teachers and whole school systems are incapable of becoming more relationally effective?[23]

The understandable—and laudable—concern about the effects of positive and negative school relationships on children should not eclipse the significant effects relationships have on practicing teachers. Andy Hargreaves found that relationships with students were the most important sources of enjoyment and motivation for the teachers; he also found that conflicted or alienated relationships tended to diminish both teachers' professional satisfaction and their personal sense of well-being. Another Dutch research team conducting a review of studies of how teachers are affected by student-teacher relationships confirmed that relationships carry a clear reciprocal impact. They observed that the "emotional labor" of teaching renders it as among the most stressful occupations. Research into the phenomenon of "teacher burnout" further corroborates the toll taken when teachers feel themselves held fast in challenging relationships with students, especially when the teacher has already internalized negative impressions of a resistant student.[24]

CHAPTER THREE

■ ■ ■

The Promise of
Relational Teaching

IN OUR UNDERSTANDABLE CONCERN about some children's failure to thrive, we too easily forget that children are eminently resilient. Buoyed by secure attachments to nurturing adults who invite engagement in purposeful activity, children reveal an encouraging ability to overcome adversities and meet challenges of all kinds. School classrooms, rightly conceived, offer relational resources that enable students to deepen their engagement while overcoming whatever standing resistance, setbacks, or uncertainties they bring with them to school.[1]

For centuries, Western societies in particular have generated the largely unexamined assumption that boys are inherently school-averse, and prevailing cultural expectations have made this aversion more likely. But, as we have indicated, boys show a remarkable acceptance of the value and necessity of their school programs. When asked, boys express a deep appreciation of teachers who make an effort to get to know them and help them to succeed. As we will document, the teachers whom boys single out for praise combine relational skill with an impressive mastery of their subjects and an adherence to high but attainable standards.

Positive teacher-student relationships are not merely an affectively pleasing value added to instruction. In relationship, boys relax their defenses, accepting the invitation to engage and to try; the pleasures of expanded awareness, new facility, and competence are amplified because they are shared. With various degrees of eloquence, students of all types and ability reported the elevating experience of *learning in relationship*. As one Australian boy acknowledged:

> Having a positive relationship makes you enjoy the subject. I become relaxed and cooperate better in class. I am able to joke with my teacher and that creates a better environment for the both of us. We respect one another and we know the limits. When I go to this subject, I feel motivated, excited, and . . . willing to be educated.

Successful teaching and learning do not occur in a mechanistic transmission of instruction and content from teacher to student, but rather in an emotion-charged relational medium created by teachers' directive presence, resulting in a climate in which students' engagement, effort, and ultimate mastery are mutually embraced aims. School performance improves when children are engaged in the right kind of relationships with their teachers. The relational imperative, however, comes with a kind of Zen-ish caveat. For while the evidence suggests overwhelmingly that positive relationships result in encouraging improvement in student conduct and achievement, that improvement will prove elusive if the imperative to "be relational" is read by students—boys, in particular—as a mere stratagem to get them on track. Relationships flower into engagement and productivity only when teachers authentically experience their students as valuable, likable, interesting beings: as ends, not means.

Observations such as this American boy's summary of his relationship to a favored teacher indicate the contours of an effective relationship:

When I started my first year with her, she made an effort to get to know me in the first few lessons. This really did make the bond between us as a student and teacher very strong. We are in a professional relationship where friendly jokes are part of the lesson, whether it is [my] demonstrating her idiosyncrasies in a friendly way, or [her] insulting the way that I talk. It is not malicious behavior—it is just two people who have a positive relationship . . . making a learning environment less stressful by sharing personal stories.

The "professional" relationship described by this boy is an example of a *working alliance*: collaborations in which change is sought by students, and teachers serve as the agents of change. These purposeful alliances are forged when the boy sees that his teacher, coach, or advisor genuinely knows and respects him, monitors his progress, and intervenes when necessary with effective correctives, creating a safe climate for offering comment, asking questions, revealing confusion, and seeking help.[2]

The working alliance is composed of *dyadic* exchanges between boy and teacher in the service of a *triadic* enterprise in which boy and teacher are allied in the boy's effort to master scholastic content. Although the findings suggest strongly that the triadic enterprise—boy, teacher, subject matter—is dependent on the quality of the dyadic relationship, it is equally true that a positive dyadic relationship is unlikely to be formed in the absence of pedagogical mastery on the teacher's part. Thus, in scholastic settings, merely warm relationships—however valuable in themselves—do not ensure success in the triadic enterprise. Nor will the triadic enterprise succeed in the absence of a positive dyadic relationship—a teacher's subject matter and pedagogical mastery notwithstanding. As David Hawkins wrote in his thoughtful reflection on pedagogical dynamics, "I, Thou, and It," the triadic enterprise supplies purpose and substance to the dyadic relationship: "Without a Thou, there is no I. Without an It, there is no content."[3]

How does relationship affect this positive outcome? Boys' narratives suggest that the dyadic dimension, once established, fosters a willingness to engage that might otherwise be absent in students. A South African boy, new to his school, in an understated way related being helped by a teacher who noticed his reticence and helped him to establish himself:

> Miss K. was the first teacher I had and I was surprised in how she was so interested in me. I was a new kid and I wasn't expecting to receive that kind of attention. I would try to talk to my teacher and try showing the same amount of interest, but I was too shy. She was the one who helped me get used to the kind people at the school. This particular teacher helped me to become less of a shy person and made me confident in myself. My confidence in myself has allowed me to explore more things in the world. I have managed to be brighter in personality. School has become a better place than it was.

In hundreds of stories of this sort, boys told of building personal confidence, embracing formerly forbidding subject matter and activities, and developing habits of work and self-discipline that changed not just their school fortunes but their lives generally.

Productive teacher-student relationships—that is, those in which the dyadic (boy-teacher) connection is in service of the triadic (boy-teacher-mastery) enterprise—often reveal an altogether distinctive affective condition. The language and emphases expressed in both boys' and teachers' relational accounts suggest that when boy and teacher are mutually engaged in a productive alliance, there is a warmth and depth of feeling that, while in some ways like friendship and filial devotion, is not really either. Hawkins described the affective state experienced in productive teaching alliances in which students are helped to mastery and success: "What is the feeling you have toward a person who does this for you? It needn't be what we call love, but it certainly *is* what we call respect. You value the other person because he is uniquely useful to you in helping you on with your life."[4]

Boy and teacher working together toward the shared project of the boy's improvement generates a distinctive emotional resonance, a feeling state actually diminished by distracting intrusions of peer-like friendliness or filial expectations. Boys made it clear that the teachers to whom they best related were not their "friends" in the sense their peer friends were. Purposeful, mutually engaged student-teacher relationships bear their own distinctive range and quality of feeling.

In both their positive and negative relational narratives, teachers reported stepping back from standard practices and taking special measures to address the problems and needs of resistant boys, but the positive accounts documented success with boys whose patterns of resistance and unsatisfactory performance were often indistinguishable from those recounted in the negative narratives. What differed in the accounts of the successful teachers was their openness to *continuous reassessment* of their relational approaches. Whatever theory or analytic construct was initially guiding teachers in the successful accounts, when an approach did not seem to work, those teachers reconsidered assumptions and improvised a new approach.

In the negative accounts, on the other hand, once the teacher's favored remedial approach failed to achieve its intended result, there was a tendency to determine that a boy was beyond the teacher's—or perhaps any teacher's—ability to reach and to help. In their negative accounts, boys and teachers described relational failure in sharply contrasting ways. While both tended to attribute the fault and cause of relational breakdown to the other, the boys dismissed their designated teachers as professionally ill equipped and/or personally unlikable, whereas teachers often attributed relational failure to disadvantageous circumstances, such as insurmountable learning deficits, intractable psychological problems, or debilitating domestic circumstances. Unsurprisingly, both boys and teachers expressed a measure of personal hurt, frustration, and resentment in these failed relationships. From both boys' and teachers' perspectives, offense was given and offense was taken.

In chapters 9 and 10 we will examine the common features of failed relationships as they appear in teachers' and boys' narratives. Central to many of the negative narratives is a value position that assumes a boy's "buy-in" to the scholastic agenda as a necessary condition for academic or relational success. Teachers who took this position assumed their classes would typically include a cohort of underperformers and failures, attributed to the kinds of extramural factors just cited. One New Zealand teacher's insistence on at least a *mutual* commitment to the triadic enterprise was echoed by many others discussing relational disconnection:

> A successful teacher-student relationship requires mutual commitment from student and teacher. The student's motivation level is the most apparent factor in creating an effective teaching relationship.

Failing this essential motivation and a measure of good will on the boy's part, little hope was extended for the possibility of relational connection, with characteristically grim results. Such was the experience of one South African teacher:

> In the Bloomsbury English dictionary *relationship* is defined as "the connection between two or more people or groups and their involvement with one another, especially as regards the way they behave toward and feel about one another." In analyzing "relationship" between students and teachers this is an important definition, especially the "behave toward . . . one another" part of the definition. In this instance, the boy concerned was not particularly overtly confrontational or awkward, but was completely dismissive and very deceitful in the way in which he went about it. It was this latter attribute, especially, which made it very difficult to deal with and made [me] feel that it was something being very intentionally mounted against [me]! One of his particular approaches was to talk under his breath to one of the other boys on his table and then to start grinning . . . and looking sideways at me, appearing to be making a mockery of me. When [the boy was] challenged about it [he replied] that it was nothing related to the class and [asked] why was I bothering about it! Over an extensive period of time, so I realized later, he would arrive and pass wind and the whole class would be disrupted.

While establishing an expectation of civility and decency is appropriate, if not essential, on a teacher's part, the likelihood that every boy who enters the classroom will arrive with those characteristics is low. Teachers' accounts of relational success included many instances of boys' progress from disengagement to engagement, opposition to cooperation, in consequence of a series of relational gestures made by the teacher. The unsuccessful relational narratives, by contrast, included more instances of teachers' closing off relational possibility in response to a boy's oppositional behavior, as in this account by another frustrated South African teacher:

> He simply refused to work, and deliberately set out to be class clown —I found him subversive and he constantly attempted to sidetrack my teaching. I tried the good cop–bad cop approach with him, and appealed to his better nature at first. I then tried harsher measures, but nothing worked. In the end, for the sake of the class I simply marginalized him and got on as if he wasn't there at all. The irony was that he was a very capable boy and a really brilliant sportsman who in many ways was the ideal schoolboy. I got to the stage where I actively disliked this boy, whom I frankly thought of as an arrogant, spoilt brat who had received too much praise for his sporting prowess too young. In retrospect he probably sensed this, which would account for the tension between us. Teaching this boy was an unpleasant experience, and I was glad when the academic year ended. He was one of the very, very few boys that I have taught who did not say goodbye or leave a present when he finished the year—hardly surprising really, but still it showed.

Few veteran teachers have not encountered a student who might qualify as an "arrogant spoilt brat," and we have no evidence to challenge the aptness of that assessment in the preceding account. But as Michael Nakkula and Sharon Ravitch at the Graduate School of Education of the University of Pennsylvania have cautioned, such assessments create a "forestructure of understanding" that prompts and guides a teacher's subsequent responses to a student.[5]

When teacher-student relations reach an impasse, both parties are stuck. In the course of reviewing more than two thousand written narratives and in our on-site focus groups and workshops with teachers and boys, we did not hear of a single instance in which a boy, on his own initiative, was able to repair a relational breakdown with a teacher. In every instance of an unlikely relationship being created or a ruptured relationship repaired, the teacher improvised and executed the necessary relational gestures, as in this South African teacher's reckoning with a boy's bad reaction to a minor disciplinary measure—denying the boy the use of a calculator on a mathematics test.

> As I thought about it, it became clear to me that my denying this student the use of a calculator had coincided with his significant effort to prove to me that he was trying his best. He had wanted to show me that he could succeed in my subject. Knowing him as I did it became clear that unless I confronted the issue he was unlikely to go to such lengths again for me. After thinking through the issue I went out of my way to find him. I asked him . . . how he was feeling about the incident. I explained to him the reasons I had not immediately offered him the use of my calculator but also empathized with the way he was feeling. I told him that I appreciated the preparation that he had put into the test and suggested a way in which he could do an alternate test. This approach was greatly appreciated . . . as he realized that I also wanted the best for him. The fact that I went out of my way to find him also made him realize that I was concerned for him. He did far better in the re-test and continues to work very well in my class a year later now. He often goes beyond what is expected of him and I regularly commend him for this. Had I not realized the impact of what I thought was educationally the right thing to do at the time, by not allowing him use of my calculator, it is likely that this relationship would never have produced the positive fruits that it continues to do.

In characterizing the teacher-student relationship as a working alliance, we extend a fundamental concept from psychotherapy to the field of teaching and learning. Without overstating their similarities, both psychotherapy and teaching represent collaborations in which a common endeavor unites the participants. In describing the warmth, mutuality, and purposefulness of boys' relationships with teachers, we find the concept of working alliance helpful in a couple of ways. First, it explains boys' deep appreciation and respect even for teachers whose outward manner may not be notably "warm" but whose dedication and mastery are noted with gratitude and affection. Secondly, the working alliance implies a division of roles and responsibilities that can help both student and teacher monitor and maintain the relationship when it shows signs of stress or breakdown.

Both positive and negative relational narratives composed by boys included many instances of their own resistant and obstructive behavior in class. A defining feature of the positive accounts, however, was that the teacher in question assumed the responsibility of *relationship manager*. The working alliance paradigm we propose assumes that the student, especially if challenged by the material, emotionally conflicted, or fearing failure, is less free and less able to maintain an objective perspective on the partnership. Accordingly, it falls to the teacher, professionally trained and better able to resist personalizing resistance and opposition, to establish and maintain productive connection.

In his paper proposing the working alliance as an apt construct for teaching, Daniel Rogers stated that the teacher assumes three responsibilities not shared by the student: (1) to serve as the expert facilitating the student's learning, (2) to maintain an overall awareness of the alliance, and (3) to monitor and mend strains in the alliance. In our study, relationally successful teachers did not *expect* students to assume mutual responsibility for an improved working alliance in the classroom.[6]

Teachers should also not expect, nor should they wait for, resistant or underperforming boys to seek help when they are unable to master assignments. Rather than personalizing the impasse, relationally successful teachers understand that many factors bear upon a boy's ability to enter trusting relationships. With the help of colleagues and willing parents, teachers working to identify the extramural factors bearing on the student's resistance are often able to improvise new strategies to forge a more productive alliance.

Relationally skilled teachers develop a repertoire for inviting each student into the working alliance. In the following chapters we will consider the specific relational gestures successful teachers extend to their students, noting that such gestures are always provisional. If a particular strategy or approach fails to achieve the desired connection, relationally deft teachers improvise another. Relationally successful teachers understand that at any given moment they do not—and cannot—know all that they need to in order to generate desired improvement in a boy's conduct or scholastic performance. As Miriam Raider-Roth has written, "The hardest part of this [relationship-building] process is knowing ourselves as teachers. This requires keeping a close eye on what we can see, what we shut out, and what our responses sound like to our students."[7]

One of the defining differences in the positive and negative relational accounts submitted to us is that in the positive narratives teachers acknowledged a need to change their own interpretations and practices in order to elicit change in their students. By contrast, the negative accounts were dominated by expectations on the part of teachers that, given the unquestioned validity of various assumptions, it was up to the student to change. The acknowledgment that relational success and subsequent scholastic success require *both* teacher and student to adjust can be unsettling and temporarily uncomfortable, especially for accomplished, veteran teachers. Nakkula and Ravitch have asserted the necessity of *mutual* change for successful relationships of all sorts, including teaching relationships: "A central assumption of this model is that counselor engagement necessitates counselor change—not a comforting assumption for those of us with set prescriptions for treatment, for those of us who believe that our training is complete."[8]

While an imperative to see beyond one's blind spots may seem oxymoronic, Raider-Roth reminds teachers that assistance in transcending limiting perspectives lies very near at hand: "We cannot see our blind spots without our colleagues' gentle and persistent feedback. We cannot see the complexity of children without viewing their worlds from multiple perspectives."[9]

School leaders, too, can help teachers to exercise continuous reassessment of their assumptions and practices by openly acknowledging that *every* teacher—master or novice—experiences relationship frustrations and snags at some point. In creating a climate where collaboratively reviewing relational possibilities and difficulties is normative, a climate in which teachers are eager to share rather than hide relational challenges, schools stand to advance both morale and scholastic achievement.

A pervasive theme running through the positive relationship narratives is that they are *transformative*; in consequence of the relationship, boys' behavior changed and scholastic improvement followed, sometimes dramatically. A related finding is that this transformative efficacy does not depend on unevenly distributed gifts, as is too often suggested in popular school fictions that celebrate the eccentric or specially gifted individual as the only effective relationship maker in an otherwise deadening scholastic community. On the contrary, our findings suggest that relationship making is a fundamental human capacity; it is *developable*. That the same relational gestures succeeded in so many different school settings and were reported with such consistency by teachers of all disciplines, by both early-career and veteran teachers and by male and female teachers, strongly suggests that there is no single relational "type" or personality. Relationally successful teachers reveal a determination to improvise until a climate is established in which the boy is able to make eye contact and engage in spoken exchanges both in and outside of class, a climate in which school matters and other matters of common interest can be comfortably aired and shared.

Our findings indicate that once their resistance is understood and overcome, boys enter readily and warmly into relationship with their teachers, and it is essential that teachers honor their vulnerability in so doing. In this regard teachers must take care that their own needs for warmth and intimacy do not drive the triadic enterprise off course. Schools worldwide are working to establish legal and institutional guidelines for appropriate adult-child relationships. The heightened contemporary concern about adult violations of children's trust, including physical and sexual abuse as well as emotional manipulation, has generated a great deal of highly specific conditions bearing on how, when, and where teachers and students can interact in and outside of school. These understandable concerns are overall a heartening indication of a larger moral commitment to children's welfare.

But these new initiatives may also foster an unhelpful climate of unease and caution as educators consider the necessity of improving and deepening relationships between students and teachers. The caution is due to the fact that exploitative adults often conceal their actual intentions within *appropriate* relational gestures—they are kind and helpful to the children they approach; they initiate contact, listen, and make themselves available in multiple settings. Adults intent on taking advantage of children succeed because they appear to meet—and perhaps for a time actually meet—children's relational needs.

The confusing fact of the matter is that relationally skillful teachers will make the same kinds of relational gestures that exploitative adults might make in their initial interactions with children. But the findings of this study draw a sharp distinction between relational efforts designed to forge effective learning alliances with students and those intended to serve adults' own needs. The relational gestures that succeed with boys *enable learning* and can ultimately be evaluated on the basis of observable improvements in boys' engagement, productivity, and performance. For teachers, relational success resides in the student's deepening engagement and growing mastery of the subject matter addressed in the working alliance. By contrast, teachers who cultivate student relationships in order to meet personal needs have lost sight of the developmental and educational aims of the working alliance. However motivated, such teachers attempt to forge peer-like relations with students, which, given the authoritative role of the teacher, create both boundary confusion for students as well as opportunities for them to be emotionally manipulated and even abused.

Teachers confronted by student resistance stemming from gender, race, and socioeconomic and other cultural factors face special but by no means insurmountable challenges. Relationally successful teachers recount how cultural differences often enrich rather than diminish relational possibilities—openly shared perspectives providing a *mutually educative* opportunity for both student and teacher. Teachers in this study who conveyed a genuine curiosity about a boy's particular cultural attitudes and circumstances reported an unexpected willingness on the part of boys to share their experiences—and a corresponding relief at no longer having to defend themselves against preconceptions and stereotypes. Teachers willing to acknowledge the concerns—even seemingly unwarranted ones—that students confide to them about feeling isolated in a majority culture have already passed through the threshold of a promising relationship.

Committed teachers may be fortified by our finding that the transformation of boys' resistance often takes *extended time*—weeks, months, sometimes multiple school terms, sometimes years. In actual school practice, single cathartic episodes are rarely the occasions for positive change. Unlike popular fiction and films, dramatic confrontations and cathartic moments appeared to play little part in advancing the developmental and scholastic fortunes of the students participating in this study.

■ ■ ■

CHAPTER FOUR

Conveying Mastery and
Maintaining Standards

WE WERE STRUCK WHEN first reviewing the survey returns that the boys were by quite a margin more willing than their teachers to attribute relational success to a teacher's mastery of their pedagogy and adherence to high but attainable standards. While, again, they were appreciative and grateful for their teacher's relational attentions, there was nothing particularly warm and fuzzy about their assessments. The boys assumed implicitly that their shared enterprise with their teachers was a scholastic one in which they were supposed to benefit. The teacher's ability to establish relationship was clearly the threshold to their productive engagement, but that engagement was sustained by their teachers' persuasive mastery of the subject taught as well as their ability to create a stimulating and emotionally safe classroom climate.

Boys cited teachers who made them feel confident that, despite prior setbacks, they would succeed and who established clear pathways to improvement and success. Boys noted warmly the effort—the preparation and thoughtful lesson planning—their teachers expended to make their classes engaging and productive. In that purposeful climate, boys, like this South African student, become positively stimulated to meet the task at hand:

> This is the teacher who I feel I get on with the most, and I like his teaching style. He is a funny, interesting teacher, and what I like about him the most is that he is passionate about his work and approaches it in a fun and nondull manner. Instead of just constantly repeating the topic we are learning or the section we are doing, he explains it to us in one lesson and then after gives us work so that we can learn by practice and not theory. He pushes me beyond the limitations I have set for myself and literally forces me to go the extra mile. I like a challenge and when one is presented in front of me I will do what I must to complete it. If someone else genuinely believes I can do it, then I'll do it. Also he never gives up on us. He knows that nothing is beyond my comprehension in his subject. His point of view is simply, "I've done what I can and now it's up to [you]" and I like that.

As indicated earlier, both teachers and boys attributed relational success to various ways teachers masterfully conveyed their material and maintained clear standards. This finding may serve to underscore what we mean when we describe boys' relationships with teachers as *working alliances*. While strong, positive feelings did indeed come to bear on these accounts of mastery and standard-based relationships, those feelings were elicited from boys in response to being challenged to engage, to achieve, and to *try* by teachers whose command of and interest in their material was irresistibly compelling.

The standing resistance many students carry with them into the classroom is an accretion of the uncertainties, anxieties, and remembered setbacks experienced in prior instructional settings, sometimes compounded by familial, racial, or economic hardships. The anticipated frustration of "not getting it," the shame of poor marks, of not knowing, of getting it wrong—all witnessed by an audience of peers—can be a significant barrier to engagement and learning. Relationally effective teachers took pains to present lessons worthy of boys' attention and engagement. They demonstrated at the outset of instruction that the classroom climate would be civil, respectful, and warm. They set forth clearly how to build the skills necessary to master the material and operations being taught. They let boys know how to get help and that help would be forthcoming. Finally, they established both expectations for achievement and confidence in boys' ultimate success.

Like a number of boys, this American high school boy was moved to something like awe by the meticulous care his English teacher had taken to ready his students for his class, including composing exhaustive study guides for each student—a personal investment that stimulated the boy to do his very best work.

> My teacher distinguishes himself because of his inspiration from a purely academic standpoint. Twice I have had the pleasure of enrolling in his classes, and both times he has inspired me to put forth nothing but my highest achievement. I believe that this inspiration stems from his complete and infallible mastery of the subject matter, his unflinching passion for the material, and his willingness to reach out to me personally.
>
> While most of the papers that filled my backpack on the first day of freshman year came in the form of heavy textbooks and notebooks, he handed me an especially thick packet to add to my collection. After perusing the packet I found that he himself had compiled notes on every single piece of literature in the class, each grammatical issue, extra notes on punctuation, guidelines for formal papers, and instructions for quotations and citations applicable to every piece of writing I could imagine. When I enrolled with him again my junior year, he impressed me with a spiral-bound book even more comprehensive than the one from freshman year. Confident of the breadth and depth of my teacher's knowledge, I was even more comforted by his passion for the material.

A crucial theme running through both boys' and teachers' relational accounts is that even as they were putting forth insufficient effort, failing to achieve, projecting an attitude of indifference or worse, *boys did not want to think about themselves or to have others think about them this way.* Whatever their prior history of success or failure, the boys we met with harbored hopes to do well. Relationally effective teachers succeeded in convincing resistant learners that they were capable of meeting and even exceeding expectations. As many boys in many scholastic situations attested in this study, "[The teacher] knew I could do it even when I was almost sure I couldn't." The ability of teachers to locate, to *expect* a boy's best effort, even before it has been made manifest, was a recurring feature of relationally successful practice.

This chemistry teacher in an American high school recounted the far-reaching consequences of distinguishing between how a boy presents himself at any given moment and how he might be at his best:

> A noisy and crowded classroom with students pressed around the front desk could not hide the fact that this one student just handed in his pathetic lab. I was not surprised by the work because the boy was as disheveled as the paper. His clothes, his demeanor, and his discipline were without guidelines. Sometimes a boy's original character defect involves a lack of maturity, other times it involves selfishness. This student had a problem with direction. He didn't know what he was doing in my class; he didn't know why he was there. I decided to find out who he was and in doing so perhaps he could find who he was.
>
> I asked him to see me after class. He acknowledged [that] with the slow roll of the eyes and sag of the shoulders, a look that seemed very practiced. He had the look of a person who had been taken to task before. I was not sure of what to say but I wanted to see how things would play out.
>
> At 1:30 he approached my desk . . . I fished through the pile of papers and found his lab. In a stack of typed graphs and papers I found

his mess. It was half a page of scribbled ink with the tags of ripped spiral paper dangling.

I handed him his paper and said, "Is this who you are?" I said, "Make a decision today because if this is who you are, then fine, but decide who you are." I handed his paper back to him and he took it. I told him to either redo the paper or just hand the same one in, but next class [he] must decide who [he is].

. . . Two days later, this boy enters the class and hands in a paper that is unlike his old work in every way. It is organized, it is neat, and the lab is six pages long type with graphs and comments. It is changed. I look at him and accept it and say, "So this is who you are; good."

. . . It was years later that I received an e-mail from [the boy], who was in his fourth year of medical school. He told me that it was that day eight years ago that I forced him to change. It was at that moment eight years ago at the front desk that he made a decision as to who he was.

Relationship building may begin, as it did in this instance, with confrontation. It also may begin in a teacher's adhering to standards a boy is declining to meet. This is especially likely to be the case when the boy comes to understand that the teacher's insistence that he meet the standard is not an impersonal professional principle but an expression of the teacher's concern for him. Such was the lesson recounted when this American English teacher drew a line between what was acceptable effort and what was not with a promising young writer he happened personally to like:

I had a clearly bright and verbally talented student who was always polite and pleasant but who simply would not do his homework . . . I warned him over weeks that he could not continue in an AP [Advanced Placement] class if he didn't do his work. He always apologized, always promised to do his work, and never did. At first I encouraged him [and] praised his off-the-cuff in-class work (which was very good when it did not depend on out-of-class work). The kid liked me and I him—but he simply didn't have the habit of homework and refused to acquire it . . . After several clear warnings, I finally told him he was out of the class. When reality finally dawned on him, he was very upset, genuinely upset—but I knew I could not go back on my word. He was moved to a regular class. I met with his angry father and with the boy [and offered a compromise] . . . If he could perform in the new class at the highest level for a grading period, if he could secure a letter of recommendation from his new teacher, and if he could both write a convincing petition letter and convince me face to face that he had changed—then and only then would he be allowed to rejoin the class. Result: he came back to AP English, never again failed to do his homework, enjoyed English more than ever (because he was prepared when he came to class), and earned a 5 [top mark] on the English AP [exam]. To this day he is deeply grateful to me for forcing him to change. And he has been extremely successful in college humanities classes.

Both in their written narratives and in their personal interviews, boys revealed a clear sense of when a teacher or coach was "on their case" because of some personal antipathy or because the teacher/coach genuinely wanted the best for them. When teachers have that distinction clearly in their own minds, they are able to impose considerable demands, correct, chastise, and even occasionally annoy and disappoint their charges without endangering productive relationship. This South African mathematics teacher managed to maintain a warm and much appreciated relationship with one of her students—by becoming at times his "nagger-in-chief."

He arrived in my class at the start of his penultimate school year, as a very good academic and a very good rugby player. At this stage I knew that I would teach this class for the last two years of their school careers. This was an excellent class, with a very sound work ethic. He, however, was the only boy in the class who was playing sport at the highest level. The majority of the class in fact had had the single focus of academics. It soon became clear, though, that he was very concerned about his academics, and determined to keep the balance. I often found myself in the position of checking with him that he was still on track academically, and that rugby was not taking over his life! He managed to maintain his high standards in both spheres for the first year, and at the end of that year he was appointed to a leadership position within the school. He was also a member of the First XV [school's top team] rugby training squad.

A short while into the new year, he ran into some trouble because of being overzealous in . . . the performance of his prefect duties. As a big, well-built fellow with a loud voice, his mere appearance was calculated to strike fear into the new junior boys. His arrival [in a place where junior boys were congregated] would prompt absolute silence. I tried to counsel him about getting the junior boys to coop- erate via respect, rather than fear, but he had difficulty in seeing my point of view. On occasion I had to speak to him even more harshly about how his image among the boys had plummeted from hero to zero directly as a result of his actions. He always listened very politely, but I felt that my words of caution were falling on deaf ears. The situation reached the stage where the headmaster called him in and gave him the weekend to reconsider his position. The fol- lowing Monday morning a subdued young man was waiting outside my office. He had written a long letter to the headmaster, and he wanted me to read it first. I realized that my opinion did count for something after all. It was a great letter.

Luckily this situation was resolved and he kept his leadership posi- tion. My role as nagger-in-chief continued for the rest of the year: "Are you sure you aren't spending too much time in the gym?" "Surely you don't need to go to rugby practice *every* day?" He fin- ished the year getting the school's prize for academics and sport. On the final day of the year he came down the passage with a rugby practice shirt draped over his arm, and said to me: "This is for you." He also handed me a two-page letter, written on foolscap. I had to be informed by one of our rugby coaches that this shirt was only given to a member of the First XV and that each boy only got one, so it was a very precious item. I will cherish the letter, particularly this paragraph:

"The common denominator in these past two years was you. I cannot begin to explain to you the service you have done me, a service that has shaped me into the man I hope to become. Whenever I was lost somehow you seemed to find me, when I was drained during rugby season you were the battery that drove me to do better, and whenever I was off-course you were the compass that guided me."

Teachers honor boys and their potential by holding them to high but attainable expectations. In the course of being challenged to do more and to do better work, not every boy sees it that way—at least not in the immediate present. Transformation and scholastic improvement are often preceded by a period of resistance in which boys test their teachers' insistence on better work and behavior. But even as they resist, underperforming boys are capable of seeing that teachers who require their best work and deportment are clearly *interested* in them and in their ultimate success. This realization on the part of a struggling New Zealand mathematics student surprised and delighted his teacher—who had been on the brink of giving up on the boy.

I have a boy in my mathematics class. He has not been particularly successful in previous years. He brought some of that negative attitude toward the subject into this year's class. One would describe him as a lazy student who is often absent from school with sporting commitments outside of what is catered for at school. His home situation is not a stable one and he alternates between spending time at mom and dad's houses.

I initially put a lot of energy into trying to motivate him to be more positive and start completing homework as it was obvious that he does have ability. He never demonstrated a "bad" attitude toward me, yet at the same time I felt that I was making little progress with him. I started following the school's assertive discipline procedures and made contact with his parents expressing my concerns. I also started issuing detentions for noncompletion of homework. During all this time I tried to emphasize the fact that I was really on his side and I was acting in his best interest. I tried to build a positive relationship knowing that the boy had it in him to achieve. Time passed by with little change.

Just when I thought that I was going to give up on him we had a class visit from the head of faculty. [The boy's] work was picked to be checked and for him to do an evaluation on me . . . He asked me after class what I thought he had written. I said that I did not think it would be too positive. To my great delight he told me that he wrote that I was a great teacher and that I had changed his mind about the importance of learning. Since then the quality of his work was much improved and he started achieving in the subject.

This made me realize the impact we have on students and that we are often do not realize the impact we have on them. The importance of having a meaningful, caring relationship with students was highlighted again.

While hundreds of gratifying transformations were recounted in our faculty and student relational narratives, most lacked "storybook" quality. Encouraging student progress is often followed by lapses and regression. Whole school terms and whole school years might pass before significant change becomes evident. Moreover, along the often arduous, indeterminate way, boys in transition may not be especially appealing, cooperative, or likable. As the narratives of broken relationships recounted in the following chapters indicate, many teachers experiencing boys' seemingly intractable resistance reluctantly cease to expend the extra effort to reach them.

As we stressed earlier, the critical factor in relationships that succeeded in spite of initial, protracted resistance on a boy's part was that the teacher assumed responsibility as relationship manager. As such, teachers did not sit back passively and merely assess the boy's relational and scholastic difficulties. Instead, when they detected a boy's affective turning away, they met with the boy outside of class, identified the concern, and proposed mutual ways to reestablish connection.

This beginning English teacher in an American school had an inclination and very good reason to give up on a sullen, uncooperative boy. As was the case with many of his colleagues worldwide, the teacher succeeded both scholastically and relationally by locating and encouraging what the boy did well while insisting on his meeting appropriate behavioral standards.

> Back in the mid-1990s, I worked with a student as his JV lacrosse coach in his ninth- and tenth-grade years; I taught him tenth-grade British literature, and I served as his academic advisor his junior year. To be frank, my first impressions of him were entirely negative. He was disrespectful to adults, his peers, the school programs, and himself. I spoke to him over and over about the importance of caring, of giving one's best effort, and [of] respecting oneself first before being able to make progress. Slowly, over time, I felt that he began to mature and apply his real talents—and he seemed to "buy in" to the school mission. Eventually, I became a strong advocate for him and remain one to this day. This period of transition was not a pleasant one, however. Nonetheless, through these sustained encounters I came to appreciate pretty quickly what a tremendous turnaround this young man had made.

> My first impression of him is that he was suspended just prior to his first JV lacrosse practice because he had been caught smoking. His physical abilities in lacrosse were weak; his conduct, atrocious. Essentially, he misbehaved during practice, preventing others from keeping focused. I dealt with his childish behavior by making him sit in "time-out"—I tried to impress upon him that playing was a privilege, one he would need to respect.

In my tenth-grade survey of British literature, this boy began the year by doing none of the assigned work. I did notice that he was often reading—just not what was assigned. He refused to annotate his text in the margins as directed. His grades were mired in the F and D range in my class.

In the winter term we got to *Romeo and Juliet* and *Macbeth*. Suddenly, he seemed to come alive. When we took our quotation identification quizzes on these texts, he consistently earned near-perfect marks, far surpassing his classmates. When he reeked of cigarette smoke, I spoke to him about appearances (he still didn't seem to care much). Eventually, I dismissed him from class, telling him he had to go shower before he could come back to class. (Fortunately, he wanted to get back to class.) His attention to detail, conscientiousness, and focus in my class skyrocketed—as did his performance and his grades. He was consistently earning A– and A marks in the course by mid-winter and through the spring.

His junior year he took AP Literature, a placement my colleagues challenged as he had continued to earn deplorable marks in his other classes his sophomore year. He earned a 4 on the AP [exam] his junior year, [and] took the test again as a senior and scored a 5. As his advisor, I saw him begin to buckle down in all his classes that year. He attended a fine college [and] subsequently earned an MA in English literature, before teaching high school English at a rival school, a position he holds today. This young man is a great resource for students who might otherwise "fall through the cracks."

Although our data were not longitudinal, it is certainly true that some of the transformations teachers work to promote are realized after their students have left school. These genuine but unseen transformations are, of course, as valuable as those teachers witness. The underlying point is that teachers' efforts can register deeply and formatively whether or not boys visibly show or otherwise acknowledge it. Taking a stand to challenge a boy's underperformance, teachers plant seeds that mature over time. This Canadian economics teacher suspected he had failed to reach a resistant boy but was surprised to learn many years later that he had not:

> This boy was the very first student I met on campus before I actually started teaching. He made a great first impression, as he greeted me with a smile, firm handshake, and welcome to our school. I later found out that he would be in two of my classes that I taught, so I was looking forward to teaching him. Eventually though, as the year progressed, he became your typical grade-ten student: he had the "too cool for school" attitude and became somewhat cocky. His marks didn't match this new attitude, which he blatantly showcased to me on numerous occasions. I felt that he was never working up to his potential and when [I] called [him] out on this, he admitted to not doing so. He was content to coast through with attitude; he was satisfied with "average marks" knowing that we both knew he could be at the top of the class. It didn't matter to him, but I took it personally: this wasn't the same guy I met a few months ago.
>
> As he moved into grade eleven, I was no longer his teacher. When he would see me, he would either be nice for the sake of being so or more often he maintained his somewhat self-centered attitude. He made it a point to make sure I knew that he was doing extremely well in school (repeatedly told me of his top-ten ranking and his high mark in math, which I taught him last year). My response to him every time this happened was that I told him that I was proud of him, but not as surprised. I continuously told him that he had the potential and that I strongly felt this since teaching him last year. For some reason, I think his views on my comments and discussions the year before were misunderstood. I think that he felt that I thought he was incapable or not intelligent. Since that time, I believe he had something to prove, which in my mind was clearly not the case.
>
> I have not taught him since, but a breakthrough came this year, while he is in grade twelve. Working out in the gym, he took the

time out of his training to talk: "Sir, I don't think I ever told you this, but I am sorry for the way I acted when you taught me in grade ten." Caught off guard, I gave him a confused look. He went on to explain how now he realizes my intentions and motive behind my teaching methods and classroom etiquette. He continued to tell me how he was apologizing for everyone in those classes as he felt a lot of the students (including him) were tying to purposely test my limits on more than several occasions. He again apologized, shook my hand, and told me that I actually was a good teacher and knew what I was doing! This meant a lot especially since this was the beginning of my career. As a new teacher, I tend to doubt my abilities and effectiveness in the classroom. I have always told myself that one day if one student ever comes back to visit and all he or she tells me is a simple thank you, then I know I am on the path to being a successful teacher. I just didn't think it would have happened this early in my career . . . ironically it came from the first student I met at the school.

■ ■ ■

CHAPTER FIVE

Reaching Out
and Responding

WHEN WE SET OUT TO survey early and late adolescent boys on their relationships to their teachers, we were more than a little uncertain what their responses would be. Our uncertainty was due in part to a prevailing assumption that boys were likely to be guarded and not particularly articulate about "relationships." It was therefore instructive and often inspiring to read boys' written narratives of their successful and unsuccessful relationships—especially when we were able to meet and talk more extensively with small focus groups in a number of participating schools. We found the boys surprisingly willing to open up to us both about what they appreciated in their teachers and what frustrated them and shut them down.

We were struck by how deeply and unquestioningly the boys—even the most resistant and oppositional—accepted the assumption that they belonged in school and that the required course of instruction set before them was legitimate. Across the cultures represented in our international sample and across various school types—independent, state-supported, parochial, rural, and urban—boys tended to accept and affirm the value of their school program. When they failed to succeed and to thrive, they attributed the breakdown to the qualities of the teachers conveying the lessons.

Similarly, when they overcame obstacles and succeeded, they were effusive in their praise of the qualities of the teachers who had guided their progress. Teachers singled out for praise were skilled relationship builders, able to make boys feel known and valued, while also establishing an emotional climate classwide in which students felt safe and positively engaged. Teachers' efforts to reach out to boys who appeared to be lacking confidence or requisite skills did not go unnoticed by those we heard from. Boys responded most warmly to teachers who knew and addressed them by their names, who were aware of their personal interests and circumstances, who made an effort to know them as whole beings and not merely students in a particular discipline. Boys who were relationally engaged with their teachers told about how they suspended resistance to the tasks set before them and how they appreciated a learning climate in which it felt safe to try and fail. Boys held in this kind of relationship tended to respond, as this American middle school boy did, with great warmth:

> One teacher was there for me more than any other. He was a nice, kind-hearted person who has always helped me and always cared. He was my math teacher and he always taught me in a way that made me feel comfortable with the material. He reached out to each student and no one ever felt like they were being left behind. If someone fell back [the teacher] would work with him until he was able to catch up. I had trouble with trigonometry, but he helped me to understand it. He couldn't make it any easier, but he did make sure I understood it. I was able to do well with the extra help. He was more than a teacher, though. He didn't just care about school. He asked about things outside of school like family life and . . . sports and things I like to do. He did it genuinely, though. He didn't just say

it and forget about it afterward. If I told him I had a basketball game that night, he would always ask how it went the next day. He was always ready to learn new things about me and he really cared about his students. I really enjoyed having him as a teacher and I bet some other kid is being treated with the same amount of kindness.

Boys with discouraging school histories or from challenging extramural contexts were in special need of relational support—and of the "calm" this urban American middle school boy said helped him overcome resistance to his least favorite subject:

> I never was that interested in history, but my teacher made it fun and interesting to learn. He interacts with me in a very calm way and engages me in class. I like to ask him questions because I feel comfortable telling him that I am confused.

Boys bring not only their learning histories but also their *relational* histories with them to class. In any given classroom there are likely to be boys whose life circumstances or schooling histories have made them wary or even relationally averse. Establishing a relationship with such a child may not happen easily or quickly, but when it is achieved, the ensuing transformation can be dramatic. This American high school student, unselfconscious about using the word *love*, writes with something close to desperation about both needing and finding relational support in his school.

> My favorite teacher loves me for who I am, not what he thinks I should be. My entire life has been filled with tears and psychological pains . . . To have a mentor, an emotional cornerstone, someone you can trust, and go to in any time of need is one of the better commodities of life. When I go to a teacher and ask them how they are the first day I meet them to the last day I see them, and actually get a thoughtful answer, [that's] a sign of a personal relationship that makes people more comfortable around each other . . . The very best teachers are the ones that can look you straight in the eye at the end of the day and tell you, "You are perfect the way you are—no matter what."

Not every relational success is dramatic. Perhaps equally valuable are small gains that combine to bolster a boy's mounting confidence that he can endure bumps and setbacks and that the most dreaded aspects of school are perhaps not so dreadful after all. Such was the experience of this Canadian student as he contended with the subject he disliked most—to such an extent it made him feel "sick, nauseated, and lightheaded."

> Through my elementary school years, physical education was my least favorite, most difficult, and simply the worst subject. I met this teacher in September of 2010 at my first grade-nine gym class. The first couple of weeks were awful; I hated it even more than ever. I felt as though my teacher just didn't know me. The truth is, for the first two months, he didn't. When he noticed I was doing very poorly on my tests and my skill level was low, things changed. My teacher started to really help me out, giving me tips, working with me one-on-one during the class. He would monitor me and make sure I wasn't having trouble, and if I did he would come over and show he really cared. Although I still did not like the subject, I did not hate it entirely. I felt as though somebody cared and knew me. My grades started to improve and I began to take a greater liking to coming to gym class. This was true even during our health unit. I disliked health the most. It made me sick, nauseated, and lightheaded. I didn't think I would make it through my first health class, but my teacher was great. He made it clear that everyone had different sensibility levels to the subject matter.

No single point became clearer to us as we reviewed boys' relational narratives than that there was no "formula" for relational success, nor was there a relational personality "type." Rather, relationships tended to succeed as teacher and boy came to see each other as distinctive individuals with signature gifts, needs, and interests. Many types of teacher personalities were noted by boys in their positive narratives, but certainly one of the most appreciated features was an easy sense of humor. Teachers who could make boys laugh—at the occasional absurdity and at themselves—managed to achieve not merely welcome relief from classroom rigor but often a deeper relational connection. This American middle school boy recounted how laughing with and at his upper elementary school teacher—a woman who, he reports approvingly, "still had part of her youth left"—eased his uncertain progress as a young reader.

> In the third grade I had difficulty with reading comprehension, and the school hired a new teacher to help the students in the learning center. This teacher was fresh out of college, so she still had part of her youth left. Consequently, it wasn't awkward to joke around with her or for her to joke around with me. I remember we would always joke around about who was going to get fat because of our obsession with Dorito chips. During our sessions she would teach me certain techniques that were tedious, but at the same time built up skills that I would need to move on to middle school and high school. I would always hate having to go to our sessions just because of all the work I had to do, but when I got there she would always make the lesson fun and exciting while having tedious elements of reading comprehension. Then she finished her master's in graduate school and became my homeroom/English teacher. Because of our previous relationship, class became fun and exciting for me. I became interested in my studies, and I felt more motivated not to let her down because she taught me for so long before. I felt as though she led me to the water and it was now my turn to drink. We always joked around about what [the] other was wearing and if my teacher or I felt offended we would always say, "It's just constructive criticism," just to set each other over the edge. We would always laugh about it in the end, making the relationship so much better.

Many of the positive relationships recounted by students were, like the one just cited, catalytic in overcoming a learning challenge, but many others described how a teacher's relational gifts enhanced an already realized strength or talent. Such was the impression of this New York City high school boy when he transferred to a more demanding school:

> When I used to be in public school, I remember that I won an essay contest in the entire New York City public school system and got

to meet Mayor Michael Bloomberg. However, when I came to this school I was actually considered one of the worst writers in my grade and my teacher determined all that. She then came to me and had a lengthy conversation that lasted until we were able to figure out a solution to my writing. If it were not for that conversation, I would not [be] as good a writer as I am today, although I could still improve a lot more. I think that before I spoke to my teacher about this I actually thought I had no weaknesses in school because I was a straight A student otherwise. My teacher actually brought out of me some of the greatest pieces that I have ever written because she was open to me for everything. I think the only way a student could actually do well in something in school is by having a more open relationship with the teacher and a more comfortable relationship with them because otherwise it feels really awkward to talk to teachers about something that is really personal. School would feel like home if students were able to talk to any teacher about something personal they would not talk to anyone else about.

A number of boys in this study seemed to draw positive comfort from their teachers' acknowledgment of their anarchic impulses. This South African boy found this to be especially true of his "kind but very naughty" middle school mathematics teacher:

In year six, my marks were good but not fantastic. I am a boarder and was meant to be learning in the prep classrooms in the evening, but I just could not concentrate. My then teacher was a kind but very naughty teacher whom we all loved (he's got more tricks up his sleeve than a fully fledged clown). I was messing around until my teacher came and told me I was almost exactly as naughty as he was when he was my age. So he helped me to do my best in my studying and he told me that if I ever ended up like him, he would shoot me. Throughout the whole year he helped me study and taught me the basics of studying. The day after he taught me his first lesson, I got a 100% for my test.

In his lighthearted acknowledgment of his student's "naughtiness," a relationally deft teacher managed to finesse the boy's surface resistance while supporting him in addressing the scholastic matters at hand. Clearly the boy felt honored to be likened to the teacher in his student days. For a tentative boy in school, a teacher's extending an interest in him beyond his role as a student of an assigned subject can be positively empowering. Being taken seriously by a thoughtful adult is an invitation to take oneself seriously. Such was the experience of this British mathematics student:

> The main thing my teacher did to build our relationship was that he treated me in a way that very few people had before. He treated me not like a world-ignorant teenager, but as an intelligent peer. Being treated as somebody who knew what they were talking about, instead of like someone to be spoken down to, made life with him as a teacher very enjoyable. My teacher encouraged discussion that often veered off course of the lesson at hand and [into] personal questions and experiences related to the matter. This welcomed me into the class and made it fun to be there. Respect is a word that is thrown around all the time by teachers, but he is one of the few teachers I have ever met who truly did respect every one of his students as if they were teachers. I can't describe how good it feels to have someone in authority treat [me] as an adult.
>
> Though I'm not adult yet; I'm just a teenager. As a teenager I've found that I'm pretty confused about how to act around family, friends, and authority figures (including teachers). Around this teacher I had no doubts in my mind how I should act. I should clearly act like myself. Whether I was having a good day or a bad day, I should be myself. I only feel that comfortable around a few people (parents being one of them). Being myself allowed him to truly get to know me in a way few people have. From being able to speak my mind and hang out in the classroom to having a serious discussion with him after school, it almost felt like he had become a second father.

The boys in this study consistently expressed the importance of being addressed, understood, and valued personally by their teachers as well as of their teacher's even-handed, respectful treatment of everyone else in the class. In doing so, teachers create a climate of emotional safety in which the boys, and no doubt all children, seem to thrive, as did this South African student in his college preparatory English class. For this boy, what the teacher did for "us" was as important as what he did for "me."

> I have a very good relationship with my grade-twelve English teacher, who has a very understanding approach [that] allows a certain amount of freedom for the students, which [we return] to him with respect. Most of the students would not even think of disrespecting him as he helps us out so much. It is not a fear of getting into trouble, but more a fear of disappointing him. He knows the ability of all his students and is always willing to help them as long as they are willing to work as hard as they can . . . He has a very positive attitude toward the students and you get the sense that he truly wants us to succeed for our own benefit. He tries his best to stay in a good mood and not take things too personally. He understands that there are certain students in the class who do not have a good work ethic and have a slight attitude problem and he handles them extremely well. He does not attack them or confront them angrily but speaks to them in a way in which they can see that he is on their side and that he wants to help them. He has made me a lot more interested in English as well as in reading and this has [had] a very positive influence on my marks.

Teachers tend to succeed relationally with boys when they come to know them beyond their scholastic performance and classroom behavior. Perhaps this should not be surprising, yet many teachers participating in this study were surprised to learn how accomplished and admirable and *likable* their students were when observed in arenas closer to their hearts than, say, their mathematics or history classroom. Many teachers indicated that their relational breakthrough with underperforming and resistant boys came about when they made a special effort to find out the boy's personal strength and built that new awareness into their working alliance.

The boys' narratives repeatedly express how energized and empowered they felt when teachers took them seriously, addressed them as they might another adult, and expressed interest in their lives and circumstances beyond the classroom. Just as most boys do not define themselves or represent themselves to others in terms of their scholastic profiles, teachers seeking to build productive alliances with their students do well to look beyond scholastic measures. An appreciative awareness of a boy's signature strengths can serve as a relational platform on which tentative and resistant boys are more likely to engage and try—because their *overall* effectiveness and value are not in question.

The boys took pains to acknowledge their appreciation of teachers who made a special effort to know them beyond their classroom roles: their personal passions and achievements, their distinctive family circumstances, hobbies, tastes, and obstacles overcome. Boys confided that they felt honored by such attentions as they were by teachers who were likewise willing to disclose themselves beyond their roles as teachers. In narrative after narrative, boys described the heightened sense of responsibility they felt to behave appropriately and to do their best work when they were in a working alliance with a dimensional *person* and not merely meeting curricular requirements. This British student relates his appreciation of an English teacher who, while demanding, "really understood me":

> [He was] possibly the best teacher I ever had. When I first met him he made a pretty scary impression. He is tall, and has a loud, imposing voice. However, that did not reflect on his personality. He was very kind, and very supportive of students. At the beginning of the year I did not usually do my assignments with quality. However, he expected much from us, and made me feel I would have to meet those expectations. When I did not, he was disappointed, and that inspired me to work harder for the next time.
>
> He really thought we could excel at English. He truly believed what he said, and treated every student equally well. In my grade-seven year I struggled . . . He helped me throughout the year and by the end of the year I had improved significantly. [Not only did I] improve

in English class, [but] he inspired me to excel in my other classes as well.

I had him as my English teacher in grade nine as well. That was the best year of English I had ever had. He always keeps class interesting by relating the material to different real-life situations. He would also talk about random things that I would never have learned before. He talked to us about Greek mythology and about his days as a high school student.

I think that relating his experiences as a student was one of the best things he had done. It made me feel he understood my situations and thoughts very well. I personally felt as if he really understood me. He understood what it was like to be a teenage boy. He always gave me help when I needed it, which I am personally very grateful for. He always promptly replied to my e-mails, helping me whenever I asked. It helped a lot that I felt like he was supporting me.

This South African boy underscores what was for him the "weird" experience of feeling compelled to do his best because he could not bear to disappoint a teacher who "went out of his way to have a relationship with each of the boys in his class":

When I was younger I had a lot of trouble concentrating and doing the work given to us, whether it was during class or for homework. When I reached grade six, our class teacher was liked by everyone. Even boys who were in the high school would visit him from time to time. He was very funny and we never had a dull lesson. If the class did well in a test or worked hard for the whole day, then he would award us with a game of soccer during last period. But the thing about him that was different from other teachers is that he just wasn't teaching us and doing his job. He went out of his way to have a relationship with each of the boys in his class, and by him doing this we felt obliged to do the work. And if we didn't do it you felt like you had disappointed him and you generally felt bad, which was weird because normally I wouldn't care what the teacher thought about me.

A Canadian boy attributed his scholastic improvement to his teacher's getting to know him well enough that they were able to establish an interpersonal "common ground":

> I think that I have had a good experience with one of my teachers who helped me in many ways. He knew what my strengths are and what I needed to work on. He knew what I was capable of, even things I was not sure I would be good at. He helped me in writing, which is something that for my whole life I have struggled with. He knew I was capable of doing better than I was and influenced me to fight through it the way he fought through cancer. After the first time he helped me with my writing, getting my thoughts out, I sought to find him and get help from him. He also had many other interests that I had, so when we talked he and I had common ground. I think [he] made a special effort to get closer to me because he knew I was smart on certain things and struggled on other parts. He forced me to do what I needed to do and knew that I could do it. I also think he changed the way I saw myself doing work.

In their positive responses to teachers who reached out to make personal connections, the boys were able to distinguish between this kind of "friendliness" and the friendly transactions they enjoyed with their age-group peers. Specifically, the boys saw their teachers' relational gestures in the context of their scholastic working alliance—the teacher as the informed, concerned manager of the relationship, the boy a willing partner in an enterprise to promote his scholastic and personal development. This Canadian boy acknowledges both the friendliness and concern he experienced on the part of a warmly attentive teacher:

> He basically took me under his wing about two years ago. I had him as a teacher twice throughout my high school career—once in grade ten for math and the other time last year in grade eleven for fitness. Nowadays he stops in the hallway to chat with me, [to] catch up on what's been happening lately and/or the Toronto Maple Leafs. We

joke around sometimes too. He may not be in the same age category as me, but sometimes it feels like it.

He wants me to persevere and excel in all my classes. He bandaged me up after I had a horrible bike accident at camp during the summer. My leg was pretty bummed up, as was my arm. After my grade-ten math exam with him, he called me into the hallway. He asked me if I smoked, at all. I didn't smoke at the time, but my parents did. So I guess their smoke stuck to my clothes and he assumed that I did. After I told him I didn't, he let me go, but that sign of courtesy showed me he cared about his students. He likes to listen when you have something to say. When he teaches he takes his time, nice and slowly, to make sure we all understand the lesson.

Both teachers and boys struck an unmistakable note of affection in their accounts of successful relationships. This Canadian boy's account of an especially favored teacher is representative of the warmth with which boys described teachers who "made a special effort to get to know me":

I had a strong relationship with this teacher since the beginning. He provides comedy to the lessons along with a good amount of seriousness and focus. After some of the lessons you would want to explore the topic more because it was so interesting. Whenever you [did] not understand the material he always made it easy for you to come up to him and ask him alone. He always made it easier to understand when you are one-on-one with him. The way he teaches just makes you want to do your best and try your hardest.

He always compliments you when you do well and supports you when you don't do as well . . . One thing that improved my relationship with him is that he had a positive relationship with my older brother. Before I even met him he had some set expectations and a positive state of mind about me. He made a special effort to get to know me even before he started teaching me, and he always encouraged me to do certain activities and sports. I tried my best to please him and to look into whatever he suggested I take part in.

He is a very fun teacher to have around and he has a good balance between having fun and being serious about teaching. He gives very useful advice that always leads you in a good way. In class he always makes the odd joke that makes you laugh and keeps you positive, engaged, and interested. Outside of class the fun side of his personality would come out. All around he is a great teacher and awesome if you get to know him.

Boys were especially appreciative of teachers willing to offer them needed remediation. From the elementary grades forward, boys aware that they have not mastered necessary scholastic skills can quickly believe that the cause is lost—that they are never going to "get it"—and thus begin emotionally armoring themselves against feelings of failure by various forms of resistance. Teachers who are able to address remedial needs while instilling the confidence that they will be met create working alliances that can extend into the student's larger life. This urban American boy was unsettled to find that what he thought was an academic strength in his previous school was, in the context of his new college preparatory school, a serious deficit:

The most positive experience I have had with a teacher was with this one teacher my freshman year of high school. Coming from a public school curriculum where I wrote all of my papers the night before the due date and got A's, I believed I was a great writer. I was horribly mistaken. The very first paper I handed into her, she handed back to me covered in red ink, saying I should meet her after class for revisions. The paper was so bad she could not put a grade on it. For the next two weeks we went over the paper, going over all of my problems with my grammar and writing conventions. My teacher showed great patience and understanding as she helped me with my writing. Over that period of time, we got to know each other very well, and I learned how to write and better organize myself in school. At the end of two weeks I turned in my paper and left her office knowing that I could not only come to her for help with my writing, but as someone who would always be there to help me out with any problems I may have inside or outside the classroom.

This Canadian middle schooler expressed his relief that his teacher, while "knowing all about" his poor prior performance, refused to label him and instead came to the relationship "with a clear mind." The teacher's ability to provide a fresh relational start allowed the student to "work hard for him" and, in so doing, to transform himself.

> My teacher is someone that was really nice to me even if I wasn't the best student the year before with a different teacher. My teacher had heard all the bad things I had done the year before but he just ignored it and came in with a clear mind. In that year I thought I behaved really well and I am very thankful for him because if it weren't for him I would still have had a bad reputation. I also think that because he was nice to me I wanted to work hard for him. I wanted to work hard and be kind to him. He respected me, and I respected him, so I would say you need to have a good relationship with your teachers if you want to succeed.

Teachers who succeed in reaching students and helping them to improve are not always aware that they are *modeling* generosity and accomplishment. Such was the effect of a middle school drama teacher on this American boy, who was not especially inclined or even able to express himself on stage:

> Over the years I got to know this teacher especially well. She gave me incredibly helpful advice about projecting my voice on stage, and very useful tips on how to memorize my lines. In the classroom she would ask me questions about the work I had submitted in an effort to get to know my writing style. I think this reflects very well on her as a teacher but also as a person; it demonstrates how caring she is of her students.

> I tried to get to know this teacher the best I could. I used to have problems with speech; I couldn't enunciate certain letters and

sounds properly. One thing I always noticed about this teacher is how well she speaks. Coming from a background in drama and theater, she pronounces every word perfectly. Since she first taught me in grade five, I have tried to emulate her way of speaking and I've made substantial progress since then.

I had never really been interested in drama or acting in plays until this teacher suggested I audition. When I finally did, she worked with me and helped me come up with a character that was properly suited to the production. Her commitment and caring for her students is truly commendable; she is still one of my greatest role models.

Taken together, the boys' narratives made clear that relational effectiveness has nothing to do with pleasantly pandering to students' anti-scholastic inclinations. The teachers most revered in these student accounts were those committed both to reaching their students and to conveying the substance of their lessons. In the following account, a South African high school boy recalls being scholastically transformed under the attentive eye of a teacher he was certain would be his nemesis. In addition to the heartening scholastic improvement the boy experienced in consequence of his relationship to this teacher, he also reveals an impressive new awareness of the prior obstacles to his engaging in classroom business. These metacognitive gains were a recurring feature of the boys' relational narratives.

My previous teacher suffered a nervous breakdown shortly after the second term began. As a result the dreaded reserve [substitute] teacher, who was past retirement age and renowned for her bad temper and strict rules, took over the lessons leading up to the end of the year.

I was a terrible student looking back to the first half of the year. I was the cause of fights mostly with this teacher who had a distaste for anything that came out of my mouth (mostly smart-arse comments or swear words) and never did any work as a result of being hyperactive. I still find it funny looking back to those early years and asking myself why nobody ever took the time to explain to me exactly what I was doing wrong, why nobody ever explained the reason behind why they were asking me to "keep quiet and sit still." Having said this, however, when my teacher arrived my life was turned upside-down. She was strict and expected hard work from everyone, yet her manner was that of a typical granny. She was kind and really liked our class. For some reason she seemed to bring a calm energy that was reciprocated by all of us hyper kids. My teacher never shouted but when she spoke we hung on her every word. Reverence for her legendary temper kept all of us in line. And yet she was the first person who told me I was not bad or stupid (that in fact I was pretty smart!), but that no one would know it if I never put pen to paper. My teacher's rule of success was setting realistic boundaries, showing us what was and what wasn't acceptable and leaving the rest to us.

At the end of the year my teacher announced my name at prize giving: a shock that was clearly evident on my face as I skulked on stage in front of all the dragons that said I was going to fail the year. Only when I was on stage did I realize I had been given the general knowledge trophy and a medal for my academic improvement.

Like the transformative "granny" just cited, the relationally successful teachers described by students were often fully aware of the range of their students' resistant behavior, but were nonetheless undeterred in asking for better things.

Again, while there was no single type of teacher identified by the boys in their positive relational accounts, the depth of transformation boys reported under the instruction of committed, thoroughly prepared, and relationally deft teachers was profound—as was this American boy's experience of his middle school science teacher.

Throughout my middle school years I had seen two science rooms on the fourth floor of my school, both stacked with chemicals and interesting scientific models. However, I had only stepped foot in one of those classrooms because there was no reason to be in the other. The teacher of the unknown classroom was a mystery to me until about halfway through the fifth grade. Ironically, the first time he had ever seen me I was peeking through the window exposing his classroom. He was lighting a table on fire, and I was beyond amazed. I was stupefied. I had always wondered what happened in that classroom and at that moment I knew. In sixth grade I would have the privilege to be in his class and be inside the classroom where the mysterious man lit tables on fire. However, there was a method to his madness and he would be the best teacher I would have for years. He wasn't just the man who set the table on fire, but he was the man who had great morals, and when he taught his students, he didn't just teach them chemistry, he taught them life lessons. He and I always had a good relationship especially because I was a frequent speaker during class conversations.

Some nights I go home and I have hours on end of homework and complain and begin to get stressed about not finishing it. In spite of all this, I am still able to just think back to what life lessons my sixth-grade science teacher taught me about persevering and never quitting. Even though he might not know it, the man who lit tables on fire would change my life forever.

CHAPTER SIX

Being a Personal Advocate

WE DISCOVERED ONE OF the most encouraging findings of our study in teachers' accounts of boys who first presented themselves as scholastic *problems*—boys especially resistant to school work and relationship. Indeed, most of the positive narratives submitted by teachers began with a frank recounting of a boy's opposition to or disengagement from classroom business. The challenges posed by these resistant boys were at times stressful and even discouraging to the teachers addressing them, but through persistence and imaginative improvisation teachers succeeded in overcoming the resistance and guiding boys to mutually gratifying personal transformations. These teachers' accounts of successful relationships are shot through with the uplift and pleasure they experienced as they solved their "problems"—as well as the pleasure of getting to know and being known by boys with whom they formed a productive working alliance.

The transformations teachers described included boys with a variety of difficulties—some of which might be considered beyond the range of standard instruction. At the heart of these stories and *preceding* the scholastic or behavioral turnaround was the teacher's willingness to address the boy's resistance directly by such strategies as meeting outside of class, addressing any special needs, and taking a personal, nonscholastic interest in him.

Teachers narrating their relational successes readily acknowledged the gratification they experienced when a difficult boy became responsive and productive, but few of these transformations came quickly or easily. More typically, progress was gradual and intermittent, assured only when the relationship became agreeable to the boy himself and the teacher's role as advocate and relationship manager was fully established. The following account, composed by a Canadian history teacher, reveals something of the serrated nature of relational progress—also the pleasure the writer acknowledges in her "sense of ownership of [her student's] success."

We spend a tremendous amount of time gathering information and data about our incoming grade-nine students, particularly those that may struggle due to social emotional concerns, learning exceptionalities, behavioral concerns, or simply having selected the wrong level of study. One of our boys was identified early on as being of great concern—being on the autism spectrum. This young man was small in stature for grade nine, stubborn, [and] bright, and yet struggles in social situations with cues and particularly with the stimulation of the boys' school environment. Change was not easy.

When he gets nervous, he talks at length about whatever interests him—regardless of the appropriateness of subject or timing. Technology is his passion. But this tendency is his greatest obstacle—his colleagues will poke fun and if not shut down, will attempt to get him going. I met him at orientation camp—it was too much for him, and we had to send him home a day early, but his tenacity showed through. He was unable to handle the stimulation and physicality of the activities, and the anxiety was too much.

I had him in my grade-nine math class. I immediately began to talk to him, meet him before class to walk him there, [and] talk to him about his computer and weekend, and I set the classroom expectations and held him to them. I would be sympathetic with his daily excuses as to why he couldn't complete work, but help and assist him to do so. I attended lunchtime peer tutoring to make sure he got work completed, and praised his ability and efforts. He was pleased that I thought he was good at math. Often, confidence is the biggest obstacle to grade-nine applied math students. I would take the time to work with him and his tutor, allowing for a debrief about his day and interests, and then would insist work got done, and it did. I would advocate for him when [he was] experiencing difficulties with other students. He would seek me out in the morning or at lunch to talk. I knew it was his way of coping with anxiety or too much stimulation in the halls. He knew what the boundaries and expectations were and he met them. I communicated regularly with [his] mom, the leadership teachers, and special education to help ensure the expectations were consistent.

He did very well that term. I would take the time to sit and chat with him at lunch if he didn't have tutoring—the cafeteria was too much for him. He was quite ill after the first day of provincial testing, so I called his mom to let him know how proud I was of his achievement the first day—so that hopefully it would alleviate his anxiety. He arrived the next day and was beaming. His transition to high school has been tough, but you see the moments of happiness and excitement in this young man—when you take the time to chat with him. His second semester has been another difficult transition, but he seeks out those he is comfortable with. I hope that he learns to engage more effectively with his peers, but there has been considerable progress and he is quite an endearing character. I look forward to working with him throughout his high school career. I probably learned more from him than he did from me.

The assumption of advocacy, sometimes an almost fierce advocacy, on the part of committed teachers is a strong theme running through these narratives. A sure sense that one has played a part in a boy's transformation clearly motivates teachers to reach out to students who are not thriving. In the following account, an American teacher of remedial English shares her determination that a boy from a racial minority who was on the brink of dismissal should get back on track. Acknowledging that she "did not really understand" the boy's struggles with school, she nonetheless determined that "the school needed to be behind him" and did all she could to help him:

> [An] African American boy who was in my eighth-grade class . . . received a letter in October from the head of the school that because he was failing English he would not be sent a contract unless that situation was turned around during the first semester.
>
> The boy was devastated, as was his mother, and I was determined to make sure that he [passed] the English course that term. As extra help sessions were not sufficient, I had the boy to my home every weekend—Saturday and Sunday for most of the day—and we read together [and] worked intensively on his English term paper including research, outlining, note cards drafts, etc. I encouraged him to write on Richard Wright as I wanted him to relate to the books he was reading and to be able to bring his own experience to his work (this boy taught me how to read *Native Son*).
>
> So much of this student's problem in school was feeling different and alienated socially, emotionally, and academically. Those weekends were a struggle, as I was a hard task master, but we worked together as a team and as we did he became more confident a learner and more enthusiastic about his task. (Obviously the warm atmosphere of a home contributed to the success of our sessions.) At evaluation time that year the headmaster remarked that I was obsessional about this boy and I agreed but added that teaching him and helping him to succeed was my proudest moment at school, and it was.
>
> The boy did graduate and went on to prep school where he felt prepared for the work, made friends, and did well. He also graduated from college. For many years his mother would call me at Christmas to thank me for helping her son to help himself. I have since lost touch with the family as I think they have moved out of the city,

but his success confirmed my sense of the importance of a committed teacher in the life of a youngster and the singular gratification that comes when you help to open doors to a student who is floundering.

I believed in this boy, I knew he was intelligent, I knew his problems, I felt his pain. I did not really understand his lack of effort and passivity, but I decided to make him prevail if he could. I thought the school needed to be behind him. I got as much as I gave, and as with many very difficult tasks the road was rough and challenging. I tried to make him believe that education would be his way out of isolation and of a sense of failure—his ticket into a successful life. I will always be gratified by the part I played in this boy's journey.

The relationships recounted by teachers in this study were by no means unidirectional gestures on the part of caring teachers to needy students. The teachers were both generous and eloquent in expressing what they learned from the boys in their charge and how in consequence their personal and professional perspectives were deepened. Such was the case for this American high school science teacher, who "cherishes" what she learned and the time spent with a student who struggled to focus on school amid family and economic pressures:

A few years ago I had the opportunity to work in a high school [that] most would describe as a "rough" school. Many of the students attending came from one-parent families or foster homes. Some of the students there came from middle- to lower-class families, struggling to even afford bus fare to attend school on a regular basis. I had this one particular student in my class [who] had a very strong exterior. He had a hard time trusting people of authority because most in his life weren't around for a very long time. His experience was summed up in one of our very first interactions when he asked me, "So when will you be leaving?" But as I did with most of my students, I treated him as a young adult, holding him to reasonable standards. I tried to draw him in with life experience both he and I could relate to. Over the course of the quarter he began to let down his guard. He went from showing up late to class to coming in on time with homework in hand. Though he kept fairly reserved, I began to feel his potential as a contributing student and member of a larger community.

On one particular day he decided to spend some time with me after school. It was then that I learned more about who he was and what he dealt with on a regular basis. He started to tell about his girlfriend and how she had recently become pregnant. Her parents were really enraged, yet this young man wanted to still be a part of both her life and the child's. He had been battling with this all semester long, and it was only then that I realized what real problems he was dealing with. Here I was, worrying about him doing his homework; meanwhile he was wondering how he was going to raise this child. It was that day that I truly observed his vulnerability.

To this day I still remember and cherish that time I had getting to understand this young man. I feel that because of the consistency I created in my classroom, along with the respect I gave him as a student, regardless of his abilities in my class, he began to see me as a role model and someone he could trust.

To strike a responsive chord in a previously unresponsive student often requires a willingness to get to know the boy well enough to determine precisely which chord that would be. The catalyst for many of the successful relationships reported in this study was the teacher's coming to know a boy's personal strengths and passions— strengths and passions often occluded by the seemingly more immediate necessity of addressing his scholastic problems. One Canadian teacher was gradually able to bring a resistant reader and writer to address those necessary skills, but only after she discovered and cultivated his gifts as a storyteller. The gratifying results of their collaboration were only possible, she concluded, "when relationship building took precedence over skill building."

The student I have in mind was referred to me by his grade-three teacher for help with reading and writing. In total he and I worked together for two years. At the beginning of our time together he was very resistant to any type of reading or writing activity, and in the course of a forty-minute class he would spend the majority of time playing with the toys in the room, hiding under his chair, asking to go to the bathroom—[and] otherwise avoiding any kind of work!

Over time, it became clear that he was a very creative storyteller and we began to explore story through puppets. We also started using the computer to research animals (a favorite topic of his) and to produce written work using PowerPoint. Phonics and word building were explored through wooden letters and magnetic words. The more I tailored the activities to the student's interests (puppets, animals) and competencies (using the computer, 3-D visualization), the more buy-in I received from this student. So although the pace of learning was slower than might have otherwise occurred, it was really important to build a relationship together.

In our second year of working together, the student's resistance to working with me had disappeared for the most part, as had his bravado around writing and reading. He stopped avoiding work or pretending that it was too easy, and was much more willing to share what he didn't know or understand. We would engage in conversations around subjects that he was interested in, and he would often ask my opinions about world events or activities happening at the school.

To summarize, then, I believe this [boy's] growing success as a student began when relationship building took precedence over skill building, and when we began to relate to each other as human beings rather than as instructor and student. More than anything else, this student needed someone to see what he was good at, to show interest in him as a person, and to believe in his potential to learn.

While establishing working alliances contributed to the scholastic success of the boys discussed in these teacher narratives, a number of teachers acknowledged other important, trans-scholastic benefits of being available for relationship with boys who badly needed one. Such was the experience of this senior teacher at an American independent school:

> I didn't teach this boy, but I got to know him because he was the sort of young man who was easy to know: he engaged adults and generally respected and admired his teachers. Through the give and take of daily life, through interactions in the hallway, at my lunch table, in my office when he'd stop by and talk, we became quite close. He became a friend, though there still was some distance: I was a faculty member and an adult, and he knew that.
>
> I think we found kindred spirits in each other. He also became friendly with my wife, and would often stop by our house to visit, [both] while in high school and later when he was home from college. His own family life was somewhat chaotic, and he was looking for support and confirmation wherever he could find it.
>
> Here's what drew us together: he felt isolated, I think, because he was gay, and at this time, some years ago, our school, indeed our society, was not as accepting as it now is of homosexuality. My wife and I were sympathetic and listened. He was experiencing fairly severe depression—as was his mother—and both of us had some knowledge of depression, if not through personal experience [then] through that of family members. So we listened. I remember we once asked him: "How are you? We mean, how are you *really*?" That may have been the first time anyone asked him such a question. He opened up. We didn't give a lot of advice. I would say that our ability to lend a sympathetic ear deepened our relationship. My wife also got to know his mother a little.
>
> I think we were helpful because of our availability, of our welcoming him. We were a safe harbor. We didn't judge. And we had time—no children, not a heap of responsibilities at school. He was also looking for adults who would approve and not condemn. We still keep in touch through e-mail.

As these narratives indicate, relationships with teachers help boys facing strong extramural pressures maintain a focus on their school responsibilities. When these pressures include homophobia, racism, or poverty, the personal investment of a teacher can help a boy fight for himself. The following account, composed by a senior administrator in an American boarding school, recounts how a committed adult builds a productive relationship by, among other things, dissolving the boundary between in-school and out-of-school:

This student came to us from a very different world. His family was Dominican, and he had grown up in a fairly rough area of New York. An alumnus of our school, who ran a basketball/academic support program, identified him as someone who had the intelligence and grit to make the leap to an independent prep school in which he would be a boarder.

For this boy and his family, his move to our school was a leap of faith, a transition much more demanding than studying in a foreign country because it involved a different world on almost every level: linguistic, economic, academic, social, even athletic. Fortunately we have a program that works to support students from traditionally underrepresented backgrounds, and those of us who helped with that program were an initial safety net for him. In the beginning he was very cautious, and he was understandably proud and at times defensive of his background. As one of the Spanish teachers, I had an immediate inroad with him as I quickly became a liaison between the school and his mother, who speaks limited English. With the difficult task ahead for him to adjust to and thrive in our school without losing his sense of who he was and where he came from, it was important for him that his family have some appreciation of what he was undertaking and of the place. I talked to his mother on the phone a great deal, and I translated all of the communications from the school (the dorm handbook, the quarterly teacher comments, etc.) into Spanish for her. I knew, because he had hinted at the fact, that every time he went home, he struggled with whether to return. We began an unspoken ritual.

When he went home, I would always drive him to the bus station. On our ride to the station, I would say, "You are going to come back. You need to come back." I would often call him at home the night before he was to return just to prod him. And I was nearly always at the bus station waiting for him to bring him back to school. He told me he really hated the bland food, so we went out to dinner in search of food he would like. Over time, he began to let me in. He shared a great deal about his family, his girlfriend back home, the hardship of feeling like he belonged nowhere anymore.

By his second year, two fellow students from the New York program arrived, and he was in the position of mentor while still walking the fragile line between the two worlds. In rides to and from the bus station or at restaurants, we would talk about differences in clothes, girls' behavior, the role of physical violence between his New York neighborhood and our school. In his junior year he wrote a piece for his Spanish class. It discussed his dual psyche, one version of himself speaking to another version. In it, he revealed how difficult it was to straddle the two worlds, and how often he wanted to give up. But he recognized that he wanted to make something of his life for himself, his mother, and his community. By senior year, this boy was really coming into his own. He was in my Spanish class, and we had lively discussions, even arguments, about his Spanish and why I wanted him to learn to spell correctly in Spanish while never taking away from the colorful way in which he spoke. He graduated, went to Georgetown University, and majored in English and Spanish, and he is preparing for the LSAT exams while he lives at home with his mom and works at a law firm. He gets in touch regularly, and nearly always ends by thanking me for those car rides to the bus and those calls home.

As I reflect on why this student was so successful at our school, it strikes me first that it is because our entire community wrapped its arms around him. A parent in the community with sons at our school took him under his wing and served as a crucial mentor to him; a teacher from New York bantered and joked constantly about the ways of New York with him; the director of our support program followed his progress and challenges closely; the admissions director took pains to find him summer work and opportunities. As for my own relationship with him, it was successful for a number of reasons. He took a chance and trusted me. His mother trusted us and gave up those years with her son so that he could grow, in many ways, beyond her. I listened and used our common language of Spanish to find common ground. Mostly, I think I tried just to be there when he was most fragile.

While the previous two teacher narratives attest warmly to the establishment of caring relationships as *preconditions* for scholastic and maturational progress, especially for boys under special pressure, both include gestures—having boys into their homes, contacting them by e-mail, transporting them from home to school in their cars—that are explicitly forbidden by state or school regulations in some countries and in different regions of the same country. These restrictions have been enacted in order to protect children from inappropriate attentions of adults, an increasingly well-documented phenomenon in contemporary life. Whatever the ideal guidelines for teacher-student contact in and out of school might be determined to be, this study's positive relational accounts suggest that the central feature of scholastically *transformative* relationships is that they are directed and monitored by teachers motivated to help students achieve shared scholastic and developmental goals. Such working alliances seek to advance the student's progress; whatever affection, satisfaction, and appreciation they generate are welcome by-products of the alliance, not the aim.

Beyond meeting their students' special needs, locating and cultivating a boy's current passion or passions was the second most frequently reported relational gesture in the positive narratives teachers submitted. Attentive teachers recounted how they were able over time to tap the energy and confidence boys bring to their favorite out-of-school pursuits and link it to scholastic endeavors. And while the measurable improvements in performance were heartening to our survey respondents, the pleasure both teachers and boys expressed in finding that common ground seems often to have been the greater benefit. Such was this American English teacher's experience when he identified a student's deep immersion in music and films:

> I taught a young man in various classes over the course of three straight years, his tenth- through twelfth-grade years. He was, and is, remarkably intelligent, though he was also anxious and a bit closed off. At the start of our first year of working together, he coasted; he was clearly used to relying on his natural insight and quick mind. He didn't always do the reading, and he preferred to sit back in class and let others do the heavy lifting. To be fair, his grades were solid and above average, but he was certainly not working up to his potential. We would speak frequently outside of the classroom, and as the scope of his interests became more and more apparent, he would drop by more and more often. We would talk music and movies, primarily, but over time literature and life slipped in there just as frequently, and when he started writing a twenty-minute-long prog-rock song about *Beowulf*, I figured I had gotten through on some level.
>
> Watching this boy test the limits of his capabilities over the next two years was the most rewarding experience of my teaching career. I don't think I've ever been more proud than the day he asked me to work with him on some difficult texts over the summer because he wanted "to be a serious reader." He roused a few of his friends to join our reading group, and we met regularly over the next few months, over coffee or dinner and also in an online forum we had set up to help facilitate our discussions. The boys blew me away—everything was entirely driven by them, and they were working on a level that put many of my grad school classes to shame. Looking back, if I added anything to their experience, I think my presence legitimized to some degree for them what they were doing and worked as a safety net of sorts. The young man who used to work through everything he was about to say in a class in advance of actually saying it no longer cared if what he said was wrong or sounded foolish; he just wanted to explore and learn.

He wrote me a letter once he graduated, and he pinpointed the moment things started to "change" for him as the walk back from our first class together as we discussed the similarities between *A Separate Peace* and *Fight Club*. I'm not surprised that the moment took place outside of the actual classroom. To be sure, our time in class over the years helped establish a crucial trust between us, but the real connections came in those moments outside of the classroom, when seemingly nothing was riding on our interaction and we could just share our interests and be our true selves. I have come to learn that boys ultimately respond to such openness in ways I could have never imagined, that they will put themselves out there just as far (and farther) as I am willing to go, and that has probably been the great lesson of my time as a teacher so far.

Acknowledging and perhaps sharing a boy's personal interests can deepen a relationship to a point where he feels free to disclose more difficult concerns. Locating a boy's personal gift, then establishing a working alliance in which that gift is more fully realized, is not only scholastically productive, it is deeply satisfying for both parties in the alliance. When this music teacher in a U.K. secondary school quite accidentally became aware of a reticent student's gifts at the piano, a collaboration began that positively transformed both of them.

This student arrived at school during year ten and was allocated music as an option subject [in the United Kingdom's state testing program]. He spoke almost no English at that time. He was a pleasant student, but shy, and was finding it difficult to make friends and was clearly frustrated at his inability to access the curriculum due to his poor language skills.

I couldn't get anything out of him during lessons really, although, as I said, he was polite. One day there were year-ten examinations that resulted in the absence of about half of my class, so I decided to turn the lesson into a jam session. The atmosphere was relaxed and I invited all students to improvise on their instrument. He put his hand up, to everyone's surprise. What then happened will remain with me forever—he went to the piano and started playing the most amazing boogie-woogie tunes—one after the other. We were all gobsmacked, as he had not shown the slightest interest or aptitude on the piano before this.

After this breakthrough he rapidly started making friends as news of his skill got around. I started working with him on his English and arranged for a piano tutor and translator so that he could adapt his compositions for the requirements of the [state testing] syllabus. This young man and I became quite friendly and he was happy to work quite late after school on his compositions, and spend many hours working on his written briefs and commentaries.

Just before his examination and assessments, I asked him to perform at a school event. He did a lot of practice, as he was a bit shy. The performance was a massive success, with the head teacher singling him out for special praise. On results day I was overjoyed to discover that he had done well enough in the written examination (in English) for him to be awarded a solid passing mark for state examination in music. This was his only university-qualifying score. Grabbing what he was good at and using that to increase his confidence was key to his becoming a more rounded, happier student with lots of friends. I wish him well and am proud that I was able to help him.

Boys' artistic, athletic, and other favored activities outside school are often unknown and unacknowledged by their teachers. Even when teachers are aware of these activities, there is a possibility that they will be seen as problematic distractions from the boys' school responsibilities. Such, for a time, was the experience of these American middle school ice hockey players, until a sympathetic social studies teacher determined he would look for the positive benefits conferred by the boys' hockey program.

Our school has been fortunate in that it regularly attracts some of the most talented ice hockey players in the metro area. A few years ago, I was lucky enough to have three young boys who, at the age of twelve, played for one of the premiere, select teams in the nation.

In my sixth-grade history class, the three of them were just average students. They were polite and respectful, and they did acceptable work, but they missed a lot of class to travel with their youth hockey team. I'd often hear from my colleagues that they were frustrated with their excessive absence and they believed the boys should be spending more time in the classroom and less time on the ice.

I, on the other hand, sympathized with the boys. I had played hockey as a boy (not at their level), and I am still a huge fan of the game. What's more, the more I talked to the boys about their hockey experience, I learned that they were learning some invaluable life lessons while they were away from school. They were learning dedication (on a level beyond the average twelve-year-old), teamwork, and sportsmanship. They were also traveling North America, often representing their school, their city, and their club at exclusive tournaments.

Thus, it was a no-brainer that I made time to see the boys play when their team hosted a tournament in our city. I didn't think it was a big deal at all. I was just a hockey fan attending a game on a lazy Saturday afternoon, but my presence at their game meant the world to them. Via their parents in the stands, I learned that I was the first of their teachers to ever take an interest in their sport, and I was surely the first to attend one of their hockey games. I even remember one of them waving during a pregame, warm-up skate.

A few weeks later, the three boys traveled to Canada for two weeks to live with a French-speaking family in Quebec and represent the United States in an international youth hockey tournament. While they were away, they took the time to send me e-mail with updates on their progress. They were so excited to have someone, beyond their teammates and parents, to share their sport with.

When they returned to the classroom, I saw a renewed effort in academics. They made sure that they had completed their assignments, and asked if there were extra things they could do to make up the time they had missed in class. They even volunteered to give a presentation to the class about sportsmanship and their time in Canada. They quickly became leaders in the classroom, modeling respect and gentlemanly conduct.

Considered summarily, teachers who took pains to build a relationship around a boy's special strength or interest found they had more to talk about and a more agreeable time doing it than they did when limited to classroom business. The mutual disclosure, warmth, and trust resulting from these interactions serve as a comfortable platform for considering scholastic matters, including the need for improvement. This New Zealand science teacher was able to parlay a senior boy's interest in kayaking and other outdoor pursuits into a thoughtful reconsideration of his approach to his classmates and to his studies:

> The relationship was established as the student in question was [enrolled in] a year-twelve class and showed the ability to learn new skills very quickly compared to his peers, then once the skill set was mastered, had a tendency to seek entertainment through verbal sparring with those around him. The class in question was not academically demanding but could push students out of their specific comfort zones regularly. The student and I both had similar interests in outdoor pursuits, kayaking, mountain biking, snowboarding, etc. So I got him and a group of his similarly interested friends involved in outdoor pursuits competitions. The members of the group were all bright, academically able, and generally good blokes.
>
> The student in question was the "roguish" element of the group and had a tendency to try [to] get away with the minimum required in his academic subjects. Changes in his work ethic and behavior in some of his classes had set in at the start of year twelve when I met him. As the relationship developed, always as a teacher/staff/coach-to-student relationship, he began to be more open and frank in his conversations as we worked on developing his skills in kayaking. He

was able to vent frustrations about issues around his involvement in other extracurricular activities and a perceived lack of relevance of a lot of the content he was learning. We openly discussed such things as satisfaction derived from work and vocational commitment, compared to lifestyle and financial security, and the many ways the balance of a person's life requires periods of plain hard work of a sometimes difficult and unpleasant nature to reach goals.

His contribution to the relationship was to commit to turning up and making an effort to support a very difficult endeavor in distance kayaking as the least experienced team member. He also possessed a wry, dry wit and an ability to recognize that everyone has their fallibilities. Instead of using his ability to recognize other peoples' weaknesses, he became more tolerant and able to work with people as his self-awareness and self-discipline matured. His relationship with his parents appeared to be a healthy, normal, and robust one. They are very supportive and realistic and levelheaded people.

The relationship functioned well for this student, I feel, because he was listened to and in the process learned to actively listen better himself. He had the support in a small way from me for his search for some direction in terms of a nonjudgmental listener who was in the second year of the relationship, not one of his teachers, but supportive of both him and his present teachers—someone with a different perspective from his parents. No wiser, just different. We had experiences of school life in common. Above all I think he made the realization that I liked him and cared how he fared, and all of his teachers did too. [This] helped him to get motivated and study harder for that last third of his year thirteen [senior year] and gain very pleasing results for himself, which in turn gained him the option of choosing entry into his preferred course for [college-level] study.

Few committed teachers would argue that reaching out to students in order to meet their particular needs is not a foundational premise of their work. However, each challenging student raises the questions of "How far and how long do I reach out?" and "Can this particular need be met by me, situated as I am in this classroom and this school?" These questions arise with special force when students are not merely unresponsive but hostile and oppositional. This high school teacher in an urban American parochial school recounts how her efforts to support and praise a disruptive student with a "short fuse" formed the basis for a transformative relationship:

> In the sixth grade, one boy was a smart kid with a short fuse. He could be pleasant and eager to please, but when something set him off—watch out! He would flip over trashcans, scream, and pace, shoving desks out of his way. A few times out at recess he would just start walking off. It seemed to him that everything I did was unfair, and it was unpredictable what would set him off. Academically he knew the material but started out a bit averse to hard work. He was disorganized and rarely arrived to class with everything he needed. All of these things resulted in his being a C or lower student in my class.

> For the first semester this boy made life difficult for me, and I would have been happy to see him go on his way—to find another teacher and another school. Yet when the end-of-the-year meeting came and we were debating what students would not be asked back, I found myself fighting for him to stay. I don't know when it happened, but over the course of the year I came to realize that he had a lot of good qualities, and the more I was able to point them out and reinforce them, the less he acted out.

> One thing I have always tried to do as a teacher is to find out what my students do well and to support them in that. So when he started playing basketball that winter, I began going to his games and cheering on him and his fellow classmates. If I couldn't make a game, I was sure to ask him about it the next day. I also started talking with him one on one after he had calmed down from an incident, [making] sure he understood why he had gotten in trouble. I also

made sure to seek him out and offer him extra help—whether that meant quizzing him for the test the next day or helping him to try [to] stay organized. Finally, I started finding out what he did well and making sure to notice it. As the year progressed he started to do better academically and also his temper tantrums became fewer and more spread out. By the end of the year I was able to see the good in him a lot more often. The summer following sixth grade, he was in my advisory for our summer program. This is where I think he finally started to really trust me. I could see that he was a good leader and let him take charge of the service trip the students were designing. [Now that he is] an eighth grader, I continue to work with him even though I do not teach him. He is a common fixture in my classroom. We have even gotten to the point where I can point out a sixth grader having a meltdown and the two of us can laugh about how that used to be him. He is by no means a straight A student, but I can't remember the last time I saw his temper get the best of him, and I think that has been the greatest way I have seen him grow.

Successful student-teacher relationships deepen as each party comes to know the other beyond the restricted role as pupil and instructor in a specific discipline. When teachers are able to facilitate this deeper awareness, gratifying and unexpected results often follow, as they did in the following account of a South African English teacher's newfound appreciation of a quiet student's emergence as an accomplished Shakespearean:

A boy nervously slid into my grade-eleven class without my even noticing. He was not a stereotypical boy in our school that, with its proud rugby history and traditional values, seems to value boys with "manly" traits such as size, strength, and an ability to make big tackles. The boy was quiet, to say the least, and seemed quite content to stay "below the radar." He came out of his shell for the first time almost two months into the year when we began our Shakespeare work for the year, *Romeo and Juliet*. And blow me down—the boy quoted a soliloquy before we even started the play. This kid clearly knew his *Romeo and Juliet*. I quoted a bit of Shakespeare back at him and we never looked back. I try to create an atmosphere in my classroom where an individual's ability to manipulate words is held in higher esteem that an individual's ability to manipulate someone smaller than himself, and he thrived on this.

He was a gifted orator (and it turns out a talented musician and lyricist) and, upon finding himself in an environment that supported his strengths, he grew in confidence to the extent that even his "macho" peers developed a sense of respect for his strengths. It was a most pleasing relationship that dispelled my earlier belief that my school only has room for the "jock." I believe he saw the environment as a safe one that was developed especially for his passion and this allowed him to come out of his shell. And I think Shakespeare and the other great poets we looked at are mainly responsible for this. I also feel I played a small part in bringing out a little of the best in this particular boy.

■ ■ ■

CHAPTER SEVEN

Establishing
Common Ground

THE STORIES BOYS AND teachers shared with us in the course of our study indicated clearly that there are multiple pathways to productive relationships. The most frequently cited features in those relationships—teacher mastery and adherence to standards, reaching out to meet special needs, responding to boys' interests and talents—have been reviewed in the preceding chapters. A number of other factors bore critically, if somewhat less frequently, on relational success.

The examples cited in earlier chapters demonstrate the relationship-building potential of teachers taking pains to locate boys' personal talents and interests and then bridging that awareness to bring fresh approaches to the boys' scholastic concerns. Many teachers also related the positive effect that sharing mutual interests had on their relationships with boys. Central to these accounts was the pleasure both teacher and boy found in their discovered commonality, as recounted by this Canadian high school science teacher:

I developed a good relationship with a student by engaging him in conversations both in and out of the classroom; engaging him in chess matches, a game I know he likes; and submitt[ing] myself to a request that I read a book he suggested. It was only once I read the book in question that we really were able to converse openly and naturally (not forced or awkward). I suppose this was our "common ground" and it was in one of his areas of expertise, which might have made him more comfortable in conversing. This relationship did little to improve his grades. Nor did it improve his behavior (he was already well behaved to begin with). What it did was create a relationship that we continue to nurture between classes and at lunch hour by discussing various "topics of the day." We both agree that it inspires us internally because we both seek out the conversations and get something positive out of it.

An American high school biology teacher reported a similar relational success—and a similar pleasure in achieving it—when she and a new student in her school discovered a musical common ground.

This boy and I first met when he was a student in my sophomore biology class. He was one of seven new boys in the upper school—many more than our school usually has. We always worry about these new boys as our school starts in grade seven. At the first advisor meeting, each faculty was concerned about his fitting in and connections to the class. I was worried too at first, as I didn't see him getting to know the boys in his class. What I did notice, however, is that he was spending more and more time in my room. At first, it was during scheduled extra help times. We found out that we had some common interests: he plays cello and I played horn. We both loved rowing. Although I was not his advisor, his mom would e-mail me about his connections at school and how we could help him feel more at home.

Funny, but when he would come by during my free block, I would be frustrated as I had so much work to do, but as the year moved on

I would really look forward to our conversations. He confided in me. Nothing of real concern—just normal teenaged stuff. I found out that he had a girlfriend whom he met in orchestra. I loved knowing more about his off-campus life—primarily his love for music. To me, knowing more about a boy's life at the end of the school day is even more important than when he is at school. He came to me one day about his lack of athletic ability during the winter season. I took a chance and suggested cross-country skiing. Much to my surprise, not only did he take my advice, but he joined the team. This awkward, new boy made some meaningful connections with the team and was seen as a member of the school community! He was trusting. He shared things about his family. I felt comfortable sharing things about mine. Today, he is a junior. We have continued this relationship and when we can we spend a free block/early morning having a conversation. He is funny, smart, respectful, warm, and willing to have a relationship with peers and adults alike. I look forward to keeping/nourishing this relationship after he graduates. I hope that he feels the same.

This American mathematics teacher parlayed his discovery of two shared interests—birth order and competitive swimming—into a longstanding relationship that he believed contributed positively to a boy's math performance:

I met this student when he entered my Pre-Algebra A section on his first day at school. This was a seventh-grade honors class designed to move at a reasonably fast pace and filled with young boys who were good at and/or excited about the subject. He was no exception. Nine of these fifteen boys, not including this one, were also my advisees. As the first semester rolled along, he showed himself to be a solid math student, but he felt a bit behind his peers at times in regard to his background or prior exposure to specific topics. He began to come to occasional extra help sessions and thus began a more meaningful and personal relationship. In discovering that he was the youngest of six siblings, I let him know I was the youngest of ten. This gave us plenty to chat about between problems. It also came out that all of his siblings were accomplished swimmers and that he was working hard to be a solid swimmer as well. He explained about his 5:00 a.m. practices before school and his evening practices as well. He was a bit surprised when I knew all about his schedule and one of his club teams. Several of my nieces and nephews also swam at a high level in high school and college.

Having found common ground outside the math classroom and spending a lot of math time together, this boy came to the end of the year feeling great about his accomplishments. He approached me near the end of that year expressing the hope he would be in my class again. Though it took until his junior year, he entered my Pre-Calculus A classroom as a similarly strong student amidst a very talented group. Over the years we had seen each other briefly on campus and talked a bit about math but mostly about swimming. The intense work ethic that helped him move through the pool, which was about forty-five minutes from school, for four hours a day also helped him maximize his growth in mathematics. His incredibly strong academic success that year helped him attract a coach's interest and gain admission to a very competitive college at which he planned to pursue an engineering degree.

Though this student was rather shy entering the school, he had an outgoing personality and was a hard-working student. He had many friends in class but was not as connected, as his main sport was not offered here. Jut as he made an effort with his peers, he was tremendous about checking in with me during his senior year. As I was one of his college recommendation writers, he updated me on his school thoughts and his progress in the pool. His willingness to seek me out or stop and talk when we ran into each other during the day made a tremendous difference in the strength of our relationship.

This veteran mathematics teacher at an Australian high school recounts how, with good humor and a stimulating sense of competition, a discovered shared interest can even transform the prospect of serving a dreaded remedial detention:

The boy concerned was in my tutor group and hence we'd meet most mornings before school. I had him in my tutor group for five years. One day he was in deep discussion with his peers in the tutor group about his Saturday detention. This discussion somehow led to what he'd rather do on Saturday—and that was play table tennis. I too had interest in this sport and asked him how good he was. His response was, "I can surely beat you, sir." I refused to take it lightly and said that might not be possible. He wouldn't give up and said that he would like to challenge me and if he won then I should take him off the Saturday detention.

While I pondered the possibility of this challenge he yelled to one of his mates, "Sure, I can beat him. I have a table-tennis table at home." I then told him that the challenge was on.

An innocent member of the tutor group asked me, "Sir, why did you challenge him after you know that he has a table at home?" I explained that I had three pianos at home and I still can't play the piano.

To cut the story short, a few weeks later on that eventful day the boy concerned organized all the tutor boys to meet at the gym and then came to get me. I walked in about three minutes later with my racquet and I sensed that I had won half the battle. I completely trashed him in front of all his mates. I even destroyed some other challengers. He had to do the detention and also report early for some general mathematics support for the rest of the term. His mother called me and inquired about his eagerness to get to his tutorial thirty minutes early every day. After I explained, she said that she loved me.

A New Zealand science teacher was struck early in his career that a chance revelation of a highly particular interest—in this case, racing cars—could spark an enduring relationship with a boy at risk for slipping away.

The boy in question was, at the beginning of the year, very happy to be at school and a very lively personality. He seemed to deteriorate in his outlook over the first few months of the school year and became somewhat difficult in his behavior. His academic results were only average. It so happened that I had on the desktop wallpaper of my computer at one stage of the year a photograph of the Formula One driver Ayrton Senna driving his 1988 McLaren Honda. The first day I used the data projector with my class and this photograph came up on the screen, this boy was suddenly ecstatic.

"Is that Ayrton Senna, sir?" he asked, and continued to ask questions about my interest in Grand Prix racing, and we struck up quite a conversation. When I told him I had sat in that very car when I was nine years old, he was quite impressed, and wanted to see the photos, which I brought in to school to show him.

Since that day the boy's behavior has improved; he always seems happy to see me and is much more enthusiastic in class. It seems to me that exposing this common interest has had a profound effect on the relationship between us.

Even at their best, teacher-student relationships are asymmetrical, in that the teacher's role is to guide and instruct, and the student's role to engage and learn. The teacher determines the scholastic expectations and serves as manager of both the course of instruction and the relationship. Despite this necessary division of roles, certain relational gestures, such as the aforementioned sharing of common interests, tend to break down what can seem to boys as the authoritarian rigidity of teacher-student expectations. One such gesture recounted by both teachers and boys in this study was the willingness, in the right setting and at the right time, for teachers to disclose something personal about themselves, a disclosure that established a welcome sense of shared experience between teacher and boy and a basis for productive relationship.

When this Canadian high school English teacher realized the source of her student's hostility was not really her but an unhappy domestic situation, she succeeded in winning his trust by disclosing something of her own family's own domestic troubles:

A grade-eleven student was showing signs of unraveling. He was disengaged in class, which manifested itself in his talking out of turn, making inappropriate comments and jokes during lessons, not completing homework, and eventually doing poorly on tests and assignments. One day I made a comment about divorce that directly related to the material we were studying. The student snapped and once again made an inappropriate comment. At this point, I asked him to go outside. I met him in the hallway and a discussion ensued about his parents' divorce. When I shared with him that I too came from a divorced family, his demeanor changed immediately. From that point on, we would chat here and there about how things were going at home. I would offer "survival tips" for managing schoolwork in a tense home environment.

At that point, his parents were living separately and he was spending a week with mom and a week with dad, which was causing him some strife. When I established a creative writing club on Wednesday afternoons, he joined, using the time to write freely about his relationships with mom, dad, and his older brother, and the tension in family. The writing exercises seemed to work on a cathartic level and the student became visibly more relaxed and happier. Later that year, he sought out my help with university applications. We'd meet at lunch to go over personal statements and admissions essays. Eventually he got into the university of his choice, a place he had expected to be out of reach. He will soon be graduating from university and I have been receiving regular updates on his progress, adventures, and successes.

The student contributed to the relationship by seeking out my help. He obviously trusted me because I had shared candid and honest stories from my childhood that I applied to his experience. He made himself available for the creative writing club despite a rigorous co-curricular schedule and made time for one-on-one writing help.

I attribute honesty and directness to the success of this relationship. It took time and effort to reach out to this student beyond the parameters of the grade-eleven classroom, but it paid off.

More than a few teachers told stories of building a relationship by intentionally stepping out of role and talking to their students with a surprising frankness. And while students addressed this way may not at first have liked what they were hearing, the teacher's willingness to relate to them in a concerned, unvarnished way conveyed a certain mutuality and respect. Such was the impact of this South African house tutor's encounters with an underperforming and unpleasant tutee:

> This was a very ordinary boy . . . His family had sent two remarkable children to the school, one a rogue who was asked to leave, having achieved status as a "legend" [top oarsman on the school's crew team] and dope smoker, and his sister who was popular, but also a little wayward. [He] wanted to be good. He was physically small, prone to sulks, and suspicious of authority.

> I came into close contact with [this boy] because I stopped [my dormitory supervision duties as housemaster in one of the school's boarding houses]. My response to stopping [dorm duties] had been to request a position as an ordinary house tutor in a colleague's house whose style I admired . . . I took a mixed-age group of boys for two years in that house. He was, I could see at our first meeting, going to be a tough one to crack. He was in year eleven.

> He had bummed along in the middle of everything, never wanting to stick his neck out. One of the first things I did in a one-on-one session was to get him to write down what he wanted from the last two years of his time at the school. We then started chatting about what "wankers, posers, and pricks" the year twelves [seniors] were.

> He played basketball in summer, despite being a better than decent cricketer, and I was teacher-in-charge, so we could at least talk "ball." He was also a mad crazy Man U [Manchester United] supporter, and that also allowed me to take a jocular, oppositional approach, with a token Bayern [rival team] leaning.

> I started to push him academically from about a month into the year—he transferred into my design class, and I knew that with see-

ing him every day, on the ball courts, in the design studio, I could see how far things could go.

After three sets of dull [scholastic] results, and a lackluster sporting performance and no cultural involvement [on his part], I stopped being nice, and started asking him whether he was either a wanker, poser, or prick—he was surprised, as I'd been quite nice until then. I walked out of his study, fully expecting an irate call from the head.

This fellow came to me two days later. He asked me to explain what I meant. I did, and he started to listen to some of the advice I gave. By the end of the year, he'd been made club captain of basketball, and a prefect. The following year, he ran just about every decision about his life past me, a bit of a pain, and after a bit, he realized and started to edit the consultations. His work ethic improved, his results went from dully poor to dully good (but good enough in the end to get into a university to do the course of his choice). His pride in his achievements [is one] of my highlights of that year. He still writes me an e-mail every couple of months to tell me how he's doing.

Boys who for social or scholastic reasons are not thriving in school often feel that they are unique in their distress—and how could a teacher begin to understand? Under these circumstances, when a teacher makes a deft personal disclosure, the boy is likely to feel less isolated. He is reassured knowing that his "problem" was also experienced by his teacher—living proof that the problem can be solved. This American middle school teacher was able to overcome a learning-impaired boy's discouragement by finding the right moment to share her unhappy past and what she learned from it:

This boy entered my class as a cheerful sixth-grade boy who was enthusiastic about middle school. Reports from the lower school had informed me that he struggled academically and testing had confirmed that he fit the profile of ADD [Attention Deficit Disorder]. His family situation had grown more challenging in recent years; his father had remarried and his mother needed to return to work full-time. His time was divided between households. Regardless of numerous challenges, he was remarkably positive and distinguished himself as a well-liked leader among his peers.

As the first grading period came to an end, it was clear that his grades didn't match his enthusiasm for learning. His homework was completed hastily or not at all. His test scores fell in the C–D range. He was soaring socially and offered excellent contributions to our class discussions, but sometimes I wondered if school itself served as a place for him to "relax" or maybe even a place where he could simply feel "safe and secure" within a day that revolved around consistency and routines.

This boy was content with Cs and Ds, but his parents were not. I spoke to his mother and offered some strategies for helping him manage his agenda and calendar. He made some real strides, but only half the time. When his scores took a dip, mom checked dates and was swift to share that low scores correlated with time at the father's house. His low grades seemed to stir tension in an already troubled family dynamic. His spirits began to sink. His test scores dropped further.

I met with him during study hall and let him know I was worried about him—that he didn't seem like himself, that I missed his insightful contributions to class discussions and could I do anything to help? He told me that he really liked middle school, but that he just couldn't keep up with the tests and homework. We discussed the success of earlier strategies, but he told me that he really needed to handle homework and test prep on his own—getting his parents involved just seemed to get them "fired up" at each other. I took a deep breath, and told him, "I get it—my parents got divorced, too." "It's really not fair," he said. "I know."

What I told him next went something like this: "You can't fix the thing with your parents and you really don't get to ask for fair—at any time in your life—but you like school, right?" He reminded me that he liked everything about school—except the tests. "So, when you're at school, you're surrounded by friends, you like learning about stuff, and you've got a bunch of teachers who want to help you succeed?" He agreed. "So, what if you look at it this way? School is a part of your life that you *do* have control over. Everything here runs on a routine. Figure out the routine [and] put some extra energy toward 'playing the game,' and I'm confident you'll see some great results."

The student was able to verbalize how that routine works. "You mean, like, how this one teacher gives a quiz every day?" "Yes. What do you need to do to prep for the quiz?" He smiled, "The homework." Even though we had been in school for ten or twelve weeks, I really think he needed to talk through all the consistencies of middle school for the "light bulb" to ignite. We decided to meet the next week to touch base. During that meeting, we cleaned out his binder and his backpack. He seemed lighter when he repacked his backpack—it was half of its original girth.

In the weeks and months that followed, his smile returned and remained. He even began to enter class and show me an improved test or quiz grade from other subject. All he needed in return was a smile and a nod, but he seemed to know that I was "rooting" for him, proud of him, and happy for him. This boy succeeded in middle school by accepting what he had, appreciating the gifts around him, and taking ownership of his academic responsibilities. Two years later, I'd still run into a tall, smiling young man on campus who would stop on his path to tell me about a book he was reading or a test score worth repeating.

Personal disclosure, sincerely offered, is an invitation to relationship. This veteran American language teacher found that stepping in practically to help a boy and his parents respond to a death in the family provided an occasion for mutually enriching personal exchanges.

This student is . . . new to my school, coming from a background of home schooling. He is quiet and though he performed fine in class, I did not really get to know him very well. Just before Christmas, his grandmother in India died. Due to the circumstances of her death,

his mom and dad had to leave immediately to deal with his grandfather and the death rites.

This student lives two blocks from me. When his mom came in early
that morning just to relay what was happening, I offered to pick up
the student every morning for school (his mom did not ask that). But
it was convenient and I was happy to do this. So every morning for
nearly a month, I picked the young man up and we drove to school
together. Though the trip is only about fifteen minutes, my student
and I developed a relationship based on mutual trust and sharing.
We shared not only about our families and lives, but we listened to
the news and discussed current events. I learned about his views
and how he thought about the world. I learned how he spends his
weekends, and who he hangs with. The student's dad is a research
scientist and his mom works with the homeless. I found out that
he often goes on homeless runs with his mom during the very cold
months of the year and what he sees. He related that on one occasion, they encountered a homeless person who was very drunk,
and got a little violent when he got into the car and that [the boy]
and his mom actually took the man to the hospital and stayed with
him until he was taken care of. I often expressed to him that I had
thought about going out with them, but that I would be concerned
and afraid. As a result of conversations with my student, that homeless organization was the one I used with my students at Christmas
for a special project.

Talking to him and listening to him discuss the people they met gave
me a new view of his world. When the current news of the day reflected events in the world, my student and I discussed those events,
but we also talked about his Hindu heritage. Though my student
is not Hindu, his whole Indian family is, and so we talked about
different ways of viewing situations. We talked at length about his
grandmother's death, and the impact that will have on his whole
family. His uncle and whole family will move from the south of India
to the north to live with the grandfather. That is difficult and strange
for me to grasp, but listening to my student accept and explain that

reality was definitely a learning experience for me. As the weeks progressed, my student and I became a "mini-family" in the car every day for just those fifteen minutes. I grew to appreciate even more who the student is and he listened and learned about me. My student continues to do good work in my class. That is part of his work ethic. Though I always knew him as a great, caring kid in my class, I now see him as a very special individual who circumstances allowed me to get to know better. I am grateful for that opportunity.

There are no doubt ill-advised personal disclosures offered by teachers from time to time, particularly ones motivated by anything other than to help a student come to terms with maturational or scholastic challenges. But when they are apt, these gestures can be powerful. The boys in this study were deeply touched by and grateful for such gestures on the part of their teachers, whose disclosures were experienced as unexpected expressions of trust and respect.

Just as sharing common *interests* can catalyze teacher-student relationships, sharing common *characteristics*—race, appearance, religious affiliation—can build relationship as well. This is especially true when the student feels isolated or marginalized. Schools often fail to grasp how minority students' being thrust into an unfamiliar cultural mix can create barriers to emotional safety and scholastic focus. Many schools, especially those situated in or near urban centers, have found it easier to accommodate a diverse student body than to compose a similarly diverse teaching staff. In consequence, many students pass through their formative school years without the adult presence of someone who can relate to their ethnic experience or share their heritage. Productive teacher-student relationships can, of course, be formed across racial and other cultural lines, but when boys and teachers share an important cultural characteristic, relationships may proceed with a special ease.

In some cases, the characteristic linking a boy to a favored teacher is serendipitous, as when an American high school history teacher attributed the relational breakthrough he made to the fact that he happened to look like a troubled boy's favorite uncle. More typically, however, the realization of common characteristics united boys and teachers who shared a minority status, which was the experience of this African-born science teacher in a majority white American school:

> Being educated in an all boys' school back in West Africa many years ago, I thought it would have been a great idea to teach in an all boys' school as a way to live those memories that I missed the most. However, I had to make a connection, a connection that seemed in fact too difficult, [first] because I came from a different continent with different cultural experience and secondly [because] my students were predominately Caucasian whereas I am black.

> Despite these obstacles, after a couple of days I was able to be looked upon as the "alpha male" in the room, who had the confidence of the students to drive my biology class with great care and precision. Two students helped me do this perfectly; one of these students is a black African American young man who always had interest in what I did as a teacher. This student would set up my IT materials and even come after school to clean the screen of my laptop . . . Quite frankly, this student paved the way for me being confident that I could work in this environment.

> In fact one day the mother of this young man walked up to me in the hallway when I was hurrying for class and said . . . "My son really loves your class and he takes interest in all that you do as a teacher and as a person." I was not surprised at all, for I knew that I share common sentiments with this student. What puzzled me the most is that I did not know that this student would look up to me as a role model.

> Again, boys are just boys and sometimes they need good role models so that they can be able to follow up in all that they do. I know that I can go on and on about the different characters of boys that I meet every day in school, yet the kindness and respect that I have received from this one student is a clear manifestation of how these young men see adults and mimic their behaviors accordingly.

■ ■ ■

CHAPTER EIGHT

Accommodating
Opposition

AS NOTED IN PREVIOUS chapters, there are multiple pathways to productive teacher-student relationships. Some successful relational gestures may seem to run mildly counter to others. Just as many teachers and boys attributed relational success to the teacher's upholding important scholastic standards, others formed productive relationships as a result of teachers deciding in certain circumstances to make exceptions, to overlook in a boy's performance or conduct what they might not otherwise tolerate. In these strategic instances, making an "exception" of a boy can help him see that his individuality is known and recognized by his teacher—and that *he* matters more than the general rule.

Obviously, not all student opposition can or should be accommodated by teachers, but the deft sense of when a boy's need for emotional room and comfort trumps the value of holding him to standard expectations can expedite successful relationships that would otherwise have been unlikely. This veteran American English teacher recounted how his appreciation of a talented student's literary promise persuaded him to relax a previously firm policy of requiring daily note taking:

> I had known this boy, but not in a good way, before he was a student in my English class. He had been part of a freshman science class that, as a school administrator, I had to scold because of general misbehavior; in a subtle if not insidious way, he was one of the biggest challenges for the teacher in that class. I knew from another experience with him later that same year that he was defensive, even had a chip on his shoulder. A scuffle he had had with another student necessitated my sending a warning letter home for him and also led to my talking with him about why he had been so aggressive with the other boy. I came away from that conversation with a greater understanding of his own vulnerability and sensitivity, and I think he felt better that at least his side had been heard.
>
> When he arrived in my English class the next year, I put my previous year's experience with him behind me; I hoped he would as well. Although attentive in class, he was quiet and passively defiant about taking notes. He simply would not. While I would have admonished another student for not recording points made in class discussion and lectures (how dare he?), I chose to hold back with him. I wasn't so much afraid of a confrontation as afraid of losing him in the first week of semester. In week two of the term, I asked him to see me to talk about the first paper he had written for the course, an engaging, smart discussion of musical styles and tastes. We had a rewarding conversation about a topic we both enjoyed. He was a good writer, so the opportunity to praise him helped set the direction for the months ahead. He knew I liked his writing, and it was clear he liked to write. We never talked about the events of the previous year, and only after establishing more trust with him in a second writing conference did I mention that note taking in class might help him to keep his test grades on par with his excellent composition grades. He conceded the point in the abstract if not in practice.
>
> Did he eventually take notes in class? Yes, but only in a sporadic manner. Fortunately, his test work didn't suffer as much as it might

have had he been a less able student. More important, the losses on the note-taking front were, for me, compensated for by what became an enriched student-teacher relationship. I didn't give up the cause, but I didn't let it become an obstacle in my relationship with him. In my early teaching years, I would have fought the note-taking battle to the bitter end, no matter what. I won most of those battles, but, looking back, I know that at least a few were fought at too great a cost.

A geography teacher in Canada recounted how her stressful adjustment to teaching in her new school was relieved when, in the course of a single verbal exchange, she realized that she had been "fighting the boys when neither of us wanted to":

> I had taught for seven years when I moved to an all boys' school to teach grade nine. I had had experience teaching at coed schools, [had] international teaching experience, and had taught briefly at an all girls' school in Scotland during one of my teaching placements. None of this prepared me for teaching four classes of grade-nine boys. I felt like it was my first year teaching all over again.
>
> The boys were much more physical, knocking over chairs, accidentally brushing papers off the desk and scattering them across the floor as they sat down. The noise was different—the boys were loud. They handed in assignments with no name and no staple. They forgot their pens and pencils and liked to play a game that involved a certain bodily function (I won't go into detail). I felt like I had lost control of everything. To top it off, they didn't "talk" to me. Not the way, I realize now, the girls did in my past teaching experiences; at least, not at first.
>
> Here is what I learned. The work [handed in] with no name and no staple was thoughtful and creative. The noise, you get used to. It was the antics I continued to struggle with. For example, shortly after our headmaster had given the school a "talking to" about throwing snowballs, I walked into my class after lunch only to find the boys having a snowball fight inside the classroom. They could push my buttons.

One day, the period before lunch, when they are most driven by their stomachs, I was about to reach my breaking point. "You are staying in at lunch until this work is finished" was no sooner out of my mouth when a boy in the front row tapped me on the arm and whispered, "You do know that means you will have to spend even more time with us." In that moment, everything changed. Instead of calling a class detention, I laughed. He laughed. The mood in the room changed. In that moment, I learned the importance of "a good laugh."

I had been fighting the boys and neither of us wanted to. From that moment on, I learned to relax more. Don't get me wrong, I still had to set the rules and give consequences, but my mindset changed that day. We learned to work together rather than against each other. I learned that the boys did want to talk to me; it just took them a little longer to get there. Maybe it was about building trust or finding a connection but . . . I have found that once the boys make the connection, the relationships are strong.

Resolving to endure a boy's resistance or hostility can provide an attentive teacher the time and perspective to notice and then to cultivate scholastic promise that might not have surfaced in a climate of confrontation and disapproval. Such was the experience of this New Zealand teacher of Japanese as she got to know a prickly but promising Korean student:

A Korean boy joined my year-ten class toward the end of term three a few years ago. He was transferred from his previous school because he was spending too much time with his fellow Koreans who apparently were a bad influence. My colleague at his previous school warned me about this boy's attitude and behavior being somewhat uncooperative and problematic. He appeared to be a bit sullen and because there was another Korean boy who had very poor communicating skills in English, he spent most of his class time talking to this boy in Korean for the year.

I tried to not be prejudiced toward this boy and tried to see something positive in him. He chose Japanese for one of his year-eleven option subjects and this time he had a couple of different Korean students in class to learn Japanese with. He got on well with these boys and I realized that he was quite competitive in getting better results as well as in showing some cheek that was bordering on rudeness, which was also his way of being creative with language usage. I decided to tolerate and go along with his ways as long as we were all learning things and no one was hurt emotionally or physically.

The preparation for internal assessments [was] a good opportunity to get to know students personally, as the students generally tried to communicate their more private experiences and feelings or ideas in the target language. I normally give suggestions and point out some inconsistencies in their statements. As this boy worked on his essay writing assessment, I read what he wrote and found him to be a very honest, caring person who took his responsibility toward the family very seriously. From then on, I started to see him in quite a different light. He had a very sensitive and sensible side of his personality hidden behind the cheeky carelessness that was his exterior.

By my trying to ignore his shortcomings and to focus more on his creativity and his innate intelligence, I think he was able to grow freely in this subject and able to enjoy the process as well as the end results. It was also my pleasure as a teacher.

Some teachers recounted the benefit of weighing the "absolute" value of upholding a standard against the toll doing so might take on a boy's willingness to engage and to produce. Deciding that the prospect of deeper engagement and better work made more sense than imposing discipline and penalties, an Australian teacher of high school English related the positive outcomes that followed her decision to negotiate deadlines with a student who resisted meeting them.

When this student first entered my class he presented as a disaffected and angry young man. He slouched in fifteen minutes late to the first lesson, shirt untucked and scowling. In response to my inquiry as to the reason of his lateness, he groaned, rolled his eyes, and muttered something incomprehensible.

It was obvious that his past experiences with English had been unhappy. His confidence was very low, and his automatic response to questions was to shrug, sneer, and mumble that he "didn't know/ didn't care." As his attitude and behavior was not impacting negatively the other students in the class, I decided to take a "softly, softly" approach. When he failed to hand in a number of class assignments, I defused his defensiveness by telling him calmly that, as long as he understood that he would lose marks for late submission, we could negotiate further due dates. As he has a strong sense of fairness, he was happy to be penalized, and could calmly discuss extended deadlines. He and I thus spent the whole of term one developing a calm and nonaggressive/noncombative relationship.

I discussed my strategy with his parents, and his mother confirmed that he had had a number of relationships with teachers in the past that were characterized by mutual hostility and apparent dislike. It seems that he had come to my English class prepared for a similar "showdown" with me. He was surprised and grudgingly pleased that I was not prepared to repeat this pattern. His parents were happy to accept low marks for him for term one, in exchange for the establishment of a workable relationship with me.

As he did hand in his work (albeit very late) throughout term one, his English skills improved. He is a bright and capable student and was highly gratified by a steady increase in his marks (notwithstanding the deductions for lateness). In turn, he began to participate in class discussions, chose not to sit next to students who would encourage him to disrupt the class, and tried very hard to control his impulses to call out inappropriate comments.

He continues to apply himself in English, and is now a force for good in the classroom. I have encouraged him through a variety of interpersonal strategies, including making friendly eye contact, asking him about his interests outside school, and generally conveying the impression that I like him as a person.

The success of this relationship is attributable to a number of factors. Firstly, his parents were on board and happy to accept an initial period of low marks. If his parents had insisted that I make him hand in his work on time or be punished beyond mark deduction, it would have been very difficult to establish the calmness needed to defuse his defensive attitude. Secondly, he is an intellectually capable student. When he applied himself, he was able to see a steady improvement in his marks and skills. This was very gratifying for him and boosted his confidence, which in turn impacted positively on his behavior. Lastly, I happened to personally like him. Whilst I do not let my personal response to my students get in the way of my relationships with them, it helps to feel naturally warm toward a student. I think that he can sense that I like him, and this makes him want to please me (as everyone likes to be liked).

It has been noted earlier that the full impact of teachers' relational gestures may not be immediately apparent. This American teacher of languages and leadership training recounts the positive outcomes that resulted from her decision to "put my ego aside" in order to better understand an oppositional boy who seemed to resent her presence in the school:

I had a very contentious relationship with a tenth grader whom I did not teach. This student disliked me for a couple of reasons, but the main issue for him—as he explained to me years later—was that I had broken into his culture, which was not my own due to gender and provenance. He resented this intrusion and more importantly, he perceived incorrectly that I wanted to change his world. The tension became obvious during an experiential program I was running. During several seminars on leadership that I had arranged, he was openly disruptive and belligerent. I realized that this relative stranger was incredibly angry with me, and that I had to put my ego aside to confront the issue before he ruined the program for everyone else. So, at first my goal was to put out a fire, and not to forge a relationship with a boy I may or may not teach in the future.

My initial conversation did not go well, but I was able to get across my primary point: he was unquestionably a leader. I also made sure he understood that I valued his world and that I knew he was acting out of a form of loyalty, albeit misplaced. The question I placed before him was: did he want to be a positive or a negative leader? He listened to me but he was offended by my overt criticism of his behavior. Although the situation improved over the remainder of the week, he was definitely not a fan of mine.

Over the following year, I made a point of stopping him in the halls to praise him for his successes in school and he softened a bit toward me. Once he realized I would teach him his senior year, he popped his head in my office for a chat. He explained that he had been unfair toward me and that he was looking forward to starting over the following year in class. I was delighted and let him know how brave and mature I thought he was. I felt exceedingly fortunate because even though I had made overtures to end his animosity, he is the one who made the incredibly difficult step of accepting my "extended hand."

He taught me the importance of seeking out a relationship of value with every boy that I may have contact with, and not just my own students. The following year was a resounding success, academically and personally in our class. He was one of the top students and we talked outside of class often about a variety of topics.

Today, he and I remain in touch and he updates me on his life, as well as on his peers. My friendship with him has been an incredibly rewarding experience as a teacher and as an adult. I do not credit myself for it, since I truly believe that it was his unusual willingness to break through his animosity to give me another chance. He is a remarkable young man.

Few teachers of long tenure have not encountered students who, through physical mannerisms or direct comments, have let them know they did not care for their subject and, perhaps, them. It is natural to be offended by rudeness or disrespect, but many seasoned teachers have found that by refusing to take the bait and, to the extent possible and practical, responding to unpleasantness in a calm, unthreatened manner, they are able to learn the underlying cause of the boy's unpleasantness—trouble at home perhaps, or a fear of revealing scholastic weakness—and begin to build a productive relationship. This Afrikaans teacher in South Africa managed at length to help a student succeed—in a subject that the student had been quick to tell him he "hated":

> He came to my class in the third year of high school and immediately told me he hated my subject. I told him it was fine, but the others in the class had been with me for two years and didn't seem to mind, so as long as he didn't try to influence the others, it was okay. I always made sure that he got special attention and would ask him questions I was fairly sure he could answer. He seemed to like my sense of humor and eventually came to ask me if I could explain a few concepts to him privately, which I did and then, basically because the others seemed to like being in my class and doing well, he changed and eventually got an A in my subject at the end of his school career. The year after he left school, he was asked to come back and speak to the new final-year students and then mentioned my name to tell them how I had changed his attitude and how well he had eventually done.
>
> I think things worked out well because I never felt threatened by his negative attitude and kept on being friendly and cheerful.

When a boy's resistant behavior does not impede a teacher's ability to conduct class effectively, the teacher has some leeway in considering how strictly to respond. This veteran American teacher of advanced mathematics determined that strictly disciplining a perennially tardy senior was less important than maintaining what turned out to be a mutually rewarding relationship with the boy—who, apart from his lateness, was a willing and able student. By accommodating what might on some days have been a minor annoyance, the teacher managed to establish a mock cat-and-mouse relationship with the boy that was not only productive but outright enjoyable.

My relationship with this student started when he took my Calculus BC [advanced calculus] class as a senior. I knew he had had some depression issues and had trouble finishing assignments like long papers, so I didn't really know what to expect in a math class. Happily, with a couple of exceptions, he started off the year on a high note and maintained his good work. He is a very smart young man, but I pretty much kept my distance for fear of triggering the same issues I had heard about in other previous courses. There were numerous times when he was late for class, and after a while, while I was trying to be understanding of a boy with a clear history of difficulty completing tasks on time, I was getting annoyed with this behavior. About that time, a few months into the year, I also began to uncover his sense of humor. I knew he was quick-witted and bright, but we had really not connected on that level. Soon I was feeling comfortable about reprimanding him, and he was taking it without apparent harm. Indeed, he soon became adept at flashing a very funny look at me, with one eyebrow raised, and a bit of a perturbed look on his face as if to say, "Okay, you got me, but I'm still too cool to get to class every day on time, so good luck trying to change this behavior." This was done with just enough of a smile and a twinkle in his eye that we both came to realize that this was really a great game of matching wits and ultimately just role-playing the powerful-powerless positions we respectively held. We both enjoyed it, each teasing the other about their position in the relationship. One day I locked him out of the room when he was late, and without missing a beat he promptly went through the adjoining classroom and entered our room through the connecting door. The smug, "gotcha" look on his face was priceless, and each of us had to work to suppress a good laugh.

These interactions opened up a wonderful way for us to connect, and I am happy to say we have continued a friendship right through his college years, during which time he has been very open with me about his life.

School-age boys are almost certain to experience periods of unmanageable stress, preoccupation, and moodiness. For boys in that condition, it is positively healing to enter into productive working alliances with their teachers in full command of the material presented, able to maintain a lively, purposeful climate in the classroom—a climate in which they and their classmates are known and valued personally. The boys participating in this study were effusive in praising teachers who were at once warm and firm and fair: comfortably in control. Moreover, this perceived competence and control must be in place in order for teachers to assume their necessary role in a working alliance as relationship manager.

Necessary as such pedagogical command may be, teachers—even those trying their best—may periodically be frustrated in achieving it. In the discussion of failed relationships reviewed in the chapters to follow, boys and teachers relate a number of unproductive responses on the part of teachers whose authority and intentions are thwarted by resistant students: anger, emotional withdrawal, a tendency to attribute boys' troubles to intractable psychological or social problems. Characteristic of these unsuccessful responses from teachers is the tendency to take personally the boy's resistance and rejection, to the point that the teachers become unwilling or unable to manage the relationship.

Occasionally, teachers contending with resistant students succeed precisely because they acknowledge that they are having a hard time. And while teachers may rightly wonder if revealing such vulnerability will undermine their pedagogical role, boys—including difficult ones, who know something about vulnerability themselves—may regard such gestures as appealingly honest, opening a pathway to easier communication and ultimately to a mutually respectful relationship.

A Canadian drama instructor recounts this emotion-charged instance of mutually revealed vulnerability, which in this case led both boy and teacher to relational success:

> I had taught a young man for a number of years and worked with him on shows. His talent was formidable. I did not realize, in the early years of our relationship, that he was wrestling with personal issues of some magnitude, and by the time it became apparent to me, he

had become quite lost: to us, to me, to himself. I was heartbroken at the erosion of what I had considered a special relationship.

Finally, it came to pass that the grade elevens were to share scenes, for drama class, which proved challenging as positive group dynamics were not this class's forte! The student in question, unbeknownst to me, had been exploiting the material therapeutically. The raw honesty of the final work was so breathtaking that I broke down and cried for some time. No one moved. It spoke to the general teenage angst of the boys but especially to the pain of this hurt and angry young man. I realized at that moment that I had built up my own stone façade over many months, in order just to manage the group and "discipline" this boy who "disappointed" my expectations. He gave me a gift that day; he impacted everyone in the room. A weight was lifted off of our collective shoulders: we were able to move forward much more honestly and begin to relate more truthfully with each other, more emotionally comfortable, now, with each other. This young man worked very hard to heal himself over the next few years and spoke of that moment even after graduation. I have tried since to more fully respect that beneath so much challenging behavior is a boy crying out.

Because boys' fears of exposing their vulnerability are often the cause of their relational resistance, a teacher's admission of his or her own could help to dissolve that fear. An American high school English teacher willing to reveal her own history of "many failures" helped an unhappily self-absorbed boy disclose his deepest vulnerability—with unexpected and gratifying results.

Perhaps because we are a very busy school, I have learned to use the small pockets of time around the edges—between classes or walking to lunch. The first time I spoke to this boy outside of class was at the snack bar. Although we'd just begun the semester, he'd already struck me as someone for whom school was difficult; he seemed off-center and anxious about what would be required of him in class. At the snack bar when I teased him a little about eating junk so early in the day he looked stricken, so I sat down for a minute to make sure he knew I was only joking. Over the next couple weeks I spoke to his advisor and to his former English teacher, who told me that he had a particularly strict father who never seemed to be happy with his performance at school. When he was at my lunch table I asked him questions about his family—not directly about his father but about his siblings and where they went to school and what kinds of things he liked to do outside school.

He can be very self-deprecating, but he has a wonderful sense of humor. When he said something negative about himself, I responded with how much I'd learned from my (many!) failures. I think we bonded at lunch over a mutual love of the movies. Soon after sharing a lunch table we read a play in class about, among other things, a son's difficult relationship with his father. He had become more and more confident about speaking out in class, but usually in response to my direct questions. After we'd read and discussed this play, however, he asked the class as a whole how they thought Cory, the son in the play, could better his relationship with Troy, the father. It was a heartfelt question, and I held my breath waiting to see how the class would respond.

His question came at the end of class, and several boys stayed after to talk to him one-on-one. When I watched him walk into his next class, he was surrounded! The next day I came back to this student's question, but I framed it as if it were Cory's . . . which allowed the boys, this one included, to talk about father-son relationships. I tamped down my urge to hold forth and let go of my agenda completely that day because the boys really wanted to talk about their own lives. When we had end-of-semester conferences, he spoke movingly to me about the importance of the class and how he'd felt supported by others.

This New Zealand high school science teacher was able to establish relational connection with a belligerent and uncooperative boy only when he was able to take the boy aside and confess that he regretted their hostile confrontations—because they prevented him from knowing the boy well enough to help him.

At the start of his year-thirteen course, this student was uncooperative and belligerent. He would enter the class late, noisily, and often eating—anything that he could do to elicit a confrontation from me. This went on for some weeks.

I then had occasion to be with him on a one-to-one basis when the rest of the class were involved elsewhere and I simply pointed out that I would much rather spend the energy that our confrontations took for more productive things, like preparing him for next year. I also pointed out that because of the negative relationship we had, I didn't even know what his plans were, let alone how I could help him. We talked!

CHAPTER NINE

■ ■ ■

When Boys
Cannot Relate

AT YEAR'S END IN a coeducational school visited by one of the authors, the dean tallied up disciplinary demerits by gender: the ratio was nearly one hundred to one, boys to girls. Most of the demerits were for minor infractions—dress code, lateness, incomplete homework—but the pattern was instructive. In an imbalance common in virtually every school, boys receive the bulk of teachers' negative attention, a tendency that has raised mounting concern over the past quarter-century. Myra and David Sadker's historic 1995 study, *Failing at Fairness*, proposed that in addition to "shortchanging girls," contemporary American schools were also "miseducating boys," citing boys' disproportionate share of special education placements, medical overdiagnoses, school suspensions, and other disciplinary measures as evidence.[1]

In earlier chapters we reviewed research documenting positive correlations between teacher-student relationships, student engagement, and academic achievement. We also formulated a model for relational success including specific relationally effective gestures on the part of teachers that we believe holds promise for overcoming boys' resistance, academic disinvestment, and behavioral acting out. In proposing the promise of relationship in boys' school performance, we have described how commonly masculine stereotypes can impede the recognition of boys' relational needs and capacities.

Yet despite growing evidence of the salutary effects of relationship building with boys, neither a better conceptual model nor a menu of proven relational gestures can guarantee a positive outcome in every instance. As in other human relationships, those between teachers and students are often beset by developmental, family, and socially imposed stresses. Students and teachers carry with them to class their entire lives, including their prior relational histories. In these next two chapters, we explore how these contextual and developmental dimensions show up in accounts of unsatisfying, unsuccessful relationships and what these accounts suggest for our relational pedagogy. In this chapter, we describe negative relationships from the student perspective; in chapter 10 we discuss teachers' perspectives on relational breakdowns with their students.

As we have said, we asked boys and teachers to offer an account of a positive and negative relationship in both our survey questionnaire as well as in our focus group interviews. Reviewing these accounts sequentially, we were struck by how the stories of negative outcomes differed from the positive ones. The most striking difference was the lack of congruence between how boys and teachers saw their unhappy relationships. The boys' accounts included a good deal of blaming and teacher disparagement with little assumption of personal responsibility for the relational impasse, whereas in their accounts of relational success boys frequently acknowledged the difficulties and challenges they presented to their teachers. The teachers' accounts tended to assign cause to factors beyond their professional control: irremediable learning deficits, boys' psychological problems, and domestic circumstances or other cultural factors that made it impossible for a productive working alliance to be formed. In their negative accounts many teachers took pains to convey that they had done everything that could be professionally expected of them to reach the boy, whereas in their positive accounts they celebrated the serial attempts and sustained effort they made to overcome these same circumstances.

In our study, boys' expectations of their teachers were typically very high. As one Canadian senior boy put it, "They are *supposed* to care about us and help us to learn." When such expectations go unmet, the disappointment and resentment can be profound. Boys expect their teachers not only to be pedagogically and relationally masterful, but also to be managers of the relationship: initiating contact, offering support, repairing breaches when they arise. In striking contrast to their positive relational accounts, in which they often reflected on and acknowledged the difficulties they initially posed to teachers, boys in their negative accounts acknowledged little responsibility for relational breakdowns.

Boys who have experienced unreliable and even hurtful prior relationships understandably bring a reluctance to trust adults in a position of care or authority to them, even when those adults address them respectfully and offer guidance. Boys in particular can manifest hurt and mistrust aggressively. But what may be viewed by teachers as resistance and hostility is often simply a boy's acquired stance of self-protection. Even well-intentioned teachers may conclude that it is impossible to penetrate such armor.

This New Zealand teacher's account of failing to reach a resistant boy traces a discouraging trajectory common in our data set:

> [The boy's] parents were brought in to help me and our administrators work on a plan for him. They seemed unperturbed by our observations, believing [he] "just doesn't like school. He never has, he never will. If you are looking for someone to sweep in and make a connection with him, you are wasting your time. Just teach him what he needs to know and let him be." They said that they didn't feel the need for him to be observed or counseled. Two years later, he is no longer at our school. Obviously things didn't work out for

> him here. What it came down to, I think—to generalize—is that [the boy] had a warped perception of authority. I believe he had never had anybody in a one-up position of authority care for him or love him. He equated adults with manipulators, instructors, managers, and supervisors—nowhere in that equation were humans, people capable of giving love and getting love. Adults, in his mind, always wanted something from you. This made things hard for us in the school. Since he had never learned what a good relationship with an adult looked or felt like at home, we couldn't fit into his "lifeworld" with our calls to his sense of human connectedness—he didn't have one. He mistrusted us and that fit in with his mental paradigm of the typical one-up, one-down relationship he had always seen.

In this account the compassionate teacher describes a boy with "a warped perception of authority" who would never allow teachers close enough to help him. Such boys—disengaged, prone to disobedience and even disruption—can be found in nearly every school. In practically every classroom, some boys turn away unproductively from teachers they have concluded will not care for their needs. However it may arise, boys' disconnection reveals an important fragility in their development. In fact, as Stephen Bergman has written, male development itself conduces to boys' "turning away from the whole relational mode." Boys often experience the norms, opportunities, and pressures of their gender socialization as a "relational paradox." For boys, Bergman writes, "becoming someone special often happens at the expense of being with, or nurturing, others."[2]

Without a clearer understanding of this paradox operating in male students' lives, even veteran teachers may become discouraged about reaching boys who initially reject their attention. In fact, conflicts with students are a primary source of teacher stress and can lead to teachers themselves disconnecting from relationships. The aforementioned teacher from New Zealand recognized the student's developmental fragility—"He had never had anybody in a one-up position of authority care for him or love him"—but the recognition alone failed to generate a more successful relational strategy.

Considerable scholarship over the last decade has detailed the impact of masculine social norms on boys' academic disengagement but has too quickly attributed the problem to boys' adoption of hypermasculine identities. We talked with many boys whose demeanors initially suggested a "tough guy" or "too cool for school" identity. But as they grew more comfortable and began discussing their best and worst teacher relationships, we perceived a more complex relational narrative. Whether they got stuck in a rigid refusal to learn or softened to the extent they could enter a working alliance was largely a matter of whether they had encountered a teacher who managed to reach them. Teachers' reactions to boys' masculine posturing—sometimes seeing through it to reach a resistant boy, sometimes yielding to frustration or despair—distinguished successful from unsuccessful relationships. In this way, teachers' relationships with their male students may be especially affected by masculine norms influencing the boys in their care. Just as boys may be particularly vulnerable to relational rupture, so teachers of boys may also be vulnerable to defensive disconnection.[3]

Masculine norms bearing on boyhood were not the only relational barriers recounted by teachers in our study. Collateral pressures such as family stresses and class- or race-based factors were also frequently cited, as in the following account from a New Zealand teacher:

> [This boy] came from a troubled background, with a number of schools in various parts of the country having removed him, [and his] having gone from a succession of foster homes and seeing each new home or school as just the newest in a long line of institutions. [He] was streetwise and had a number of police interventions in his background. He was physically more mature than most year-nine students [and] noisy, loud, aggressive, and smart. [The boy] lacked any stability in either home or school environments. He was a master

at avoiding work. He would not buy stationery at the beginning of the year; he would lose what was provided; he would blame others or the teacher for stealing or losing his work to cover the fact that he had not done what was required. In class he was actively subversive. He would exaggerate every instruction. "Turn around" was the signal to revolve continuously. "Please sit down" was the instruction to sit on the ground or the floor and then [loudly exclaim] that he was only doing as he was told. Every situation was open to some form of disruption. I was excessively understanding [and] polite, which annoyed him greatly but had a detrimental effect on classroom discipline, and when this became apparent to save the rest of the class I involved the school's discipline system. It seemed that he was already well known to the dean and other agencies. [He] did not reappear after one holiday break. He had run away from his latest foster home and the cycle repeated itself with another new school, new town, new start.

Many stories of relational failure sounded similar notes: boys determined to be beyond the reach of their teachers due to overwhelming circumstances in their personal lives. From teachers' stories we could see that instances of social stress, whether originating in family, peer relations, or cultural realities, has the potential to attenuate boys' relationships with their caregivers and others wishing to engage with them. The preceding teacher's account, with its grim succession of troubles and futile gestures, is echoed by many others in our study, raising the possibility for some observers that the scholastic enterprise itself is incompatible with the pressures on boys living on the social margins.

It is encouraging, then, that the transformative effects of relational teaching appear to be especially effective with boys experiencing significant stresses. Researchers studying marginalized student populations, for example, have found that positive connections between teachers and students bear favorably on student engagement and achievement. One study of marginalized students concluded that "relationship with teachers was the most salient and consistently described feature of the interviewees' experience of school."[4]

Despite this fact, teachers can be vulnerable to more pessimistic assumptions. The South African teacher who submitted the following account echoed the exasperation expressed by many others worldwide who felt that, for some "impossible to handle" boys, school work—in this case, mathematics—was "the least of [their] worries."

> This particular boy, schooled at a government inner-city boy school, was by far the most difficult pupil that I had taught. He would sleep in class, his work was always incomplete, he did not have the required stationery, and [he] was sometimes a disruption to other pupils. He was involved in issues of theft and at one stage threatened another pupil with a knife within the school premises. This pupil was impossible to handle—no amount of talking, advising, etc., had made a difference, but it all made sense when I met with his father. The boy's background had obviously shaped him into what I had experienced. His father would not take any responsibility for the boy and his acts of violence, theft, insolence, etc. In fact, I was threatened by the father and was told to "watch my back." This boy failed grade nine and was excluded from the school. On thinking about this boy, I realized that the many hardships that he had possibly experienced (possible lack of meals, involvement in gangs, poor role models at home) meant that this mathematics class may have been the least of his worries and hence his unresponsive behavior.

Prior developmental experience certainly bore on this boy's "unresponsiveness" to the teacher's efforts, and being "threatened" by the father probably did not encourage the teacher to improvise new relational strategies. But the teacher's finding him "the most difficult pupil" he had taught does not, on the evidence of our study, preclude the possibility of the boy's positive transformation. In every focus group and workshop we conducted, including with boys whose circumstances resembled the one in the preceding story, troubled and admittedly obstructive boys confided both a desire for better relationships with adults in charge and a more general desire to succeed in school. In short, we observed a striking contrast between stories of relational success and failure that had little to do with the difficulties of a boy's circumstances.

While teachers, especially experienced teachers, might fairly be expected to bring a broader perspective and more objective, professional training to bear on their evaluation of student-teacher relationships, both teachers' and boys' attempts are more or less subjective interpretations of what are often emotion-charged mutual encounters. The relational impasses described by both boys and teachers in this study illustrate vividly how irreconcilable interpretations of a mutual experience can close off one or both parties to productive engagement.

For the boys participating in this relational study, there were clear deal breakers in relationships with their teachers. In their negative relationship narratives, boys attributed the failure to achieve a working alliance to these factors: (1) the perceived inability of teachers to present course material in a clear, compelling way and to manage their classrooms effectively, and (2) the perception of teachers as disrespectful, uninterested in them personally, or unresponsive to their needs. Once established, these negative assessments served to diminish or to terminate relational efforts on the part of those reporting them.

Whether or not we should have expected it, we were surprised to read so many accounts of teachers experienced by their students as disrespectful and disparaging. This Canadian high school student voices dread—resulting in a refusal to learn—of a teacher whose "screaming" and "getting mad at us" elicited feelings of powerlessness, vindictiveness, and rage:

> When I first met this teacher I knew my mark was going to be low. In my point of view, she was so mean! She was screaming at me or my peers, getting mad at us for not doing our work when we didn't know what we were doing, and more. It really just pissed me off and I just wanted to drop the class, but I couldn't, which made

me even more pissed. So I decided I [would] just accept the nine weeks with her. This teacher did not know how I feel about her, her teachings, or her class. In fact, I didn't want to let her know how I feel. I wanted to get her fired; I was failing, plus *she didn't teach me anything*! Even if I told her I think she wouldn't give a damn. I was dying in her class, failing, and I knew I couldn't boost my mark up. I was depressed. I didn't try to improve this relationship. Well, I tried sometimes, but still the same thing [happened] over and over and over again. I think, if I tried, nothing would happen; she would still treat me and the class the same. She didn't do anything—she didn't try to help me get a higher mark. All she did was scream at us and told us to teach ourselves the work we had to do. While we were doing this, she was just sitting on the computer.

This American boy described an experience with a teacher whose angry and derogatory remarks prompted him to involve both his parents and school administrators in getting help, though ultimately to no avail. As he detailed the learning costs of this failed relationship, he sounded a note we heard frequently in these stories: vulnerability and being "apprehensive about asking for help"—especially when entering a class, as this boy did, with "low confidence in the subject."

This teacher has always had a reputation of being very aggressive. I have had many problems with her and so have my parents. She has a very negative teaching technique, where she often begins a lesson with shouting at the class. Whenever I ask for help with something I find difficult, she again raises her voice at me and overcomplicates the work. I am apprehensive about asking for help. I have low confidence in this subject because of this. My parents made it very clear to her at a parents' evening, the way we feel about her negativity, but it didn't affect her in any way as she carries on with the same teaching technique. In a lesson she often puts you down, and I often find it hard to be confident in this subject because of this. One of the parents of a student wrote a letter of complaint to the head of department about her, and about all the problems I have mentioned.

The head of department had a word with her about this, and in the next lesson she was clearly moody and angry about this as she shouted to us about this letter. A few students including myself went to see the head of department, and in the next lesson, she again shouted to us about this. On the whole, I have strong feelings against her and she's one of the worst teachers I have ever had.

No word appeared more frequently in the boys' narratives than *respect*. A perceived lack of respect characterized nearly all the failed relationships and often caused those who felt they were disrespected to "tune out" instruction, as this American boy reported doing:

There is one thing that I cannot stand, and that is lack of equal respect for all people, [whether] that be in the form of picking favorites of students who excel in a given subject, or just a lack of respect for all students. Being in my ninth-grade year, the senior year of my school, I expect to be treated like a ninth grader. Perhaps that does not make me a teacher's equal, but I do expect not to be talked down to as if I were a student of the lower school in my first year. Often if I am not treated like I am a capable fifteen-year-old, I will not take the course as seriously.

Coaches too were assessed on the basis of the respect they conveyed to their players. This American boy offered a rather philosophical assessment of a coaching approach that did not encourage his best effort:

I know in the course of my sporting career there are some coaches who have a method of telling you that you are doing something wrong in what might be seen to be a harsh or provocative way. Sometimes this may produce results, but on the other hand it normally reduces the student to a state in which he feels the opposite and wants to stop or give up on the sport and wants to displease his coach. For me this is a very unsuitable approach to coaching. The better method in my eyes would be one in which the coach praises the student for what he does right and his improvement; this makes a connection . . . that is ever so important to teaching. However, this may sometimes make the student feel satisfied and not compelled to work harder or achieve more in his sport.

Beyond disrespect, the surest barrier to relational success with a student is to offer no invitation. Many boys in our study attributed their classroom frustration to their teachers' unresponsiveness to them—their apparent lack of concern for them as individuals seeking instruction and, in some cases, extra help. This British boy expressed disappointment—even astonishment—with a teacher who simply seemed uninterested in his students: "I wonder why he chose to be a teacher if he had no . . . enjoyment from . . . children."

A relationship that did not work for me was with a teacher recently. He came across as a man who was more concerned with the subject he taught than the pupils he was teaching it to; it was almost as if he had no time or desire to connect with a single one of them. To this day I wonder why he chose to be a teacher if he had no discernable enjoyment from working with children. He made no effort to talk to, or get to know, any children outside the classroom, nor did he even seem to care if they were struggling. I never had any personal problems with him, simply because there was no opportunity to as [he] barely even noticed me. This is not necessarily a good thing, because even a problem with him would have established a rapport, but as it was there was nothing, no rapport, no connection, good or bad. And so there was no relationship to speak of, just a lack of one which presented the problem. I found that the only pupils who really got to know him were the troublemakers, as they were the ones he spoke to most, even if it was shouting. All in all I think this teacher made no impact on me and vice versa; I found that I had to work much harder at the subject consequently because I felt a lack of support from him and so I realized it was entirely down to me to achieve anything with the information that he was giving to us.

As indicated in the positive relational narratives, boys' feeling they are known and valued personally is foundational to relational connection. In the absence of that recognition on teachers' parts, relationship—and its salutary scholastic benefits—will not be realized, as this South African boy recounted:

> My first impression of this teacher was that I was just another pupil. She was there to teach maths and that was that. Often she got my name wrong—that is, when she was not ignoring me. She never made any effort to get to know me and only stopped confusing me with another boy when he left the school. My marks were dropping. She wouldn't answer my questions and in one instance, after she congratulated another boy on being selected for something when the class told her I had been as well, she simply stared at me while an awkward silence ensued.

As discussed earlier, teachers most frequently attributed their relational successes to first locating and then successfully addressing a particular student need. Central to many of these accounts was the willingness to abandon prior practice as the teacher adapts to the unique needs of each boy. In the following narratives, boys relate the dispiriting experience of failing to receive needed help. When this Canadian boy became convinced that his teacher was unwilling to help him, he could see no way forward, either scholastically or relationally:

> I felt this teacher was lazy, [was] often unprepared, and didn't really care about his student's success. He was often caught simply sitting there for an entire lesson, relying on us to learn the material without his help. It annoyed me that he wouldn't even help students during a lesson, and only cared about how fast he got through it. He never went that extra mile for any student. His tests would sometimes consist of material we hadn't even covered in class, or sometimes would have incorrectly written questions.

Boys seeking help were especially vulnerable and easily discouraged. The realization that needed help was not forthcoming figured prominently in the accounts of relational failure, as in the experience of this Canadian boy:

> I don't think he ever knew my feelings toward him because, quite frankly, he never cared. I remember vividly, one day during class, I went up to ask him a question and as I advanced toward his desk, he scolded me and told me to sit down, telling me "to go figure it out yourself." Normally, a teacher would/should be willing to help a student; but with this outburst of his, I was thoroughly unnerved and [it] convinced me that this teacher was the worst I had ever encountered. I did not do anything to improve the relationship because I knew that all my efforts would be in vain.

Boys enter their respective classrooms with a wide range of expectations, ranging from dread to high hopes for success. Underlying each set of expectations typically is an assumption that the teacher has mastered the material to be taught as well as effective methods of delivering it. For students who may have struggled in the past, there is often an additional assumption that if help is needed, it will be given. When these expectations are not met, when boys feel their teachers are not especially interested in their own subjects, much less in them, they decline to engage and relate. This American boy, for example, wrote about how his teacher's "lack of enthusiasm" made the class a "chore" in which his own motivation and interest flagged:

> Although I expected some leniency in the course, my teacher's poor attendance, tardiness, and lack of enthusiasm for the material made the class a painful chore each day. As a student, I lost all interest in the class and found no motivation to do the readings or write the best papers I could write. By second semester, my teacher had subtly surrendered to the fact that the class would not do much work, and he did the same. I recall one day when he reprimanded us for not reading, and then asked us all to open up to the reading from the previous night. As he retrieved his textbook, he remembered that he did not know what chapter we were reading, and asked us which

it was. When he asked, nobody could answer him. While I was embarrassed having not done the reading, I felt ashamed to be a part of such a lackluster class, especially considering there were other classes, both Advanced Placement and regular, that were working considerably harder and enjoying themselves much more.

Whether recounting successful or unsuccessful relationships, the boys' narratives were suffused with expectations that teachers will add to their competence and knowledge. This Canadian boy, for example, described how he came to teach himself as a result of having a teacher who seemed unwilling to do so:

> I had a science teacher last year who I did not get along with at all. He never showed up to class on time, he didn't teach his material well, and he was generally apathetic about his students. I had heard bad things about this teacher from his past students, so I wasn't expecting much but I was still optimistic. Unfortunately, his past students were proven right over the course of the year. His teaching style is dismal; he does not clearly explain things; and although this is uncommonly a complaint, he never assigned homework. This was bad for us because we were completely unprepared for tests, as we did not get sufficient practice on homework questions that he should [have] assigned. After a while I took matters into my own hands and started assigning myself homework from the textbook, but I don't feel that it should be my job to do that. Admittedly, I never really got to know this teacher very well, but that was because of his complete lack of attention for any of his students. Even when I passed him in the hall and said hello, he rarely responded and when he did, he simply nodded at me. It is a year later and it feels as if I was never taught by him. I have not spoken to him since last year, and we never speak to each other anymore. I attribute this to the fact that he does not make an effort to get to know any of his students. I can only hope that he will attempt to improve his teaching habits and his people skills, as they are currently lacking.

Many boys in our study expressed frustration with teachers whose style and delivery failed to enable their learning. This Canadian student made no bones about his disappointment with a teacher who, he concluded, had "the personality of a breadstick . . . dipped in water":

> A teacher that I do not like is my history teacher. She is simply one of the most boring people I have ever known. When she presents, she always puts boring white slides with only words, words that she reads in her dreadfully monotone voice. She doesn't even put any images to illustrate her point. She essentially has the personality of a breadstick that has been dipped in water until it becomes a soggy mess. The subject matter makes it even worse, but my main complaint is that the teacher is simply not a very good teacher, as she cannot keep my attention.

Though disappointed, the following American boy reconciled himself to a tedious science class and came to accept the teacher's limitations, even though from the outset of the course he asked himself, "How am I going to get through this year?"

> I want to share with you a story about an experience I've had with a teacher that has been very disappointing. For almost all my elementary years, I've taken science. I loved science; it was interesting, fun, new, and innovative. My liking for science changed this year when I started grade nine. In September of 2010, I meet my new science teacher. I remember my first class with him and my initial impressions. They were not good at all. He was a monotone speaking character, I could barely hear him, and [he] seemed tired, bored, and fed up with his job. I thought to myself, "How am I going to get through the year?" Well, I can tell you, so far it hasn't been easy. When I go to class some days, it moves by really slowly; other days [it's] okay, but I just feel as though since the beginning it was lacking passion, drive, and enthusiasm. Over time, I've adjusted. Today I don't feel as unhappy as I did when I started. Maybe I've been just getting used to the tone and enthusiasm of the class. What is interesting is that I have a very good relationship with this teacher. To improve my relationship, I had no choice but to accept his way and style of teaching. It isn't my preferred method, but it is what it is.

An American boy, apparently having endured his share of air-less, unengaging instruction, specified the factors in a particular teacher's approach that failed to engage and interest him:

> I think the main reason this teacher and I did not have a very strong relationship was due to his inability to captivate my interest on any level (educational, emotional, and physical). This proved a hindrance in maintaining my focus, dedication, and overall will to participate and improve. I came to this conclusion almost immediately, just from the teacher's physical presence, tone of voice, and the way he would address the class. His clothes were out of fashion, he seemed overwhelmed and mentally absent, but most importantly, he didn't sound passionate or energetic about the subject matter. This proved detrimental to my learning experience greatly, because, as I found with this specific course, if the teacher is uninterested, than I as a student have no reason to engage with the material.

In some instances, boys' inability to relate to a teacher or to the subject taught bore no personal animosity. The problem, from the boy's standpoint, was that he could not make sense of what the teacher was saying or demonstrating; the issue was poor communication. This British boy had the special grace to see the problem as a mutual responsibility, in which "both of us were trying to understand how the other worked," though acknowledging that "I practically had to teach myself":

> A relationship with my teacher that hasn't really favored me was my relationship with my year-seven maths teacher. Although my teacher was a very nice man who I got on well with outside the classroom, I could never understand anything he talked about in the lesson. I struggled for many years after with my maths due to poor understanding of my teacher on my part and poor teaching from my teacher on his part. It was a very difficult time for both me and my teacher because both of us were trying to understand how the other worked and understood. At the end of my year-seven exams I barely got a B, which was still quite disappointing, but it took a lot

of effort on my part as I practically had to teach myself, as trying to learn from my teacher was impossible. I still see my teacher around school and our relationship outside the classroom is still very easy and relaxed. However, I still doubt, if he were to teach me again, that I would understand anything.

This South African boy, while expressing compassion and even affection for his teacher, was nevertheless frustrated and disappointed by the fact that "she is not very good at teaching the subject" of geography:

At first I really thought this teacher was going to help me enjoy geography once again. Geography has always been one of my most hated subjects. I have never really found an interest in HDI [human development index] or landforms, and so I thought this teacher could really teach me to rekindle my love for geography (as it was fun in grade four doing volcanoes). Sadly, I was wrong. It's not that I dislike the teacher; in fact, she is a very nice person. It's just that she is not very good at teaching the subject. I felt as though I wasn't able to get a firm understanding of what was going on in the course . . . and I had to rely on friends to explain everything to me. This teacher was also not very reliable. A couple times I would ask to meet her for extra help, but she did not show up. She also was terrible at explaining certain things, and would sometimes give up on what she was trying to say. When it came to that (which happened frequently), she would try to get me to ask a friend. She also had no experience teaching a class (or so it seemed). She couldn't really keep a proper train of thought going. Great person, bad teacher. Although I feel bad for her, the truth is the truth and there is nothing more I can say.

Teachers' ability to establish a focused and purposeful classroom climate was a central factor in boys' openness to engage in relationship and in schoolwork generally. From the boys' perspective, effective classroom management on the part of their teachers mattered as much as their mastery of the material presented. For this concerned Australian student, a poorly controlled mathematics class was a "horror":

> In grade nine I had a horror of a year in mathematics. Having a sound year in grade eight in math, I started grade nine in the second top class. The problem was, I don't know how some kids in my class were there. They were always causing trouble. After the first week these kids were doing everything that I would call ridiculous. No detentions; no rubbish duties. No discipline! My teacher was not doing anything about it but [telling] them to stop and not do anything. He would focus so much time on the naughty kids that he would focus less time on teaching. We were learning nothing. On test days I was barely passing just on natural ability. By the time reports came in, I had to get my parents involved.

In a similar vein, this Canadian boy recounts his struggle to stay motivated in a class where his teacher lacked the "strength" and focus to command interest and attention:

> A poor teacher that I had was in grade nine when she was a new teacher to the school: she didn't seem to hold down the class with a strong presence. She also seemed to get very angry with students, and seemed to judge students. She seemed to teach some classes with experience, but for the most part she was okay with teaching lessons. I didn't seem to be very motivated and it never seemed that I would look forward to her classes. Even though she didn't seem to have the best teacher experience, she was a nice teacher [who] seemed to make the effort to help in possibly the best way she could. She also seemed to not be able to make the right choices in hard circumstances, and seemed to have a hard time with her emotions in class. I think I could have made a bigger effort to go for extra help and teacher time, but from the classes I never felt really motivated to go in after school because her teaching ways seemed to counter my learning type.

While these boys' negative accounts express a range of frustrations and critical observations, they share a striking similarity to the positive narratives: the assumption that their teachers, classes, and the school's overall program are legitimate and potentially valuable to them. As many of the previous excerpts make clear, the disappointment and even hostility boys vent about unsatisfactory teachers are due to the fact that the boys' expectations—of subject mastery; clear, lively presentation; a willingness to clarify and offer special help, to be fair, and to show personal interest and concern—were not met. Holding (if not always articulating) the expectation of a working alliance, boys regarded these disappointments as relational deal breakers.

Another instructive feature of the boys' negative narratives is that even as their resistance to the teachers they criticized hardened, sometimes to the point of nonperformance and noncompliance, they did little to consider their own responsibility for the relational impasse. This reluctance perhaps reflects their position in the working alliance: they are caught up in the effort to learn. Many school-age boys are also unable to assume relational responsibilities with adults in authority. In the asymmetric power dynamic characterizing student-teacher relations, they expect teachers to have the foresight and power to set things to right. Yet even as they misbehave and underperform, boys do not want teachers to regard them in that light. Their overriding hope, spoken or unspoken, is that their teachers can play the part of relationship manager while they are absorbed in the challenges of learning.

In one of the vignettes recounted in this book's introduction, a senior British boy addressing an audience of teachers in a daylong workshop told a touching story of how, years earlier, his anxiety that he wasn't going to be able to learn French led to a mutually hostile relationship with a teacher who at year's end gave the boy failing marks. The boy did not dispute the marks—he acknowledged doing "garbage" work when he did any at all. When asked by the assembled teachers what he could have done to avert the failure and improve the relationship, the boy said he wasn't sure, because at the time "I was thirteen," adding that he wished his teacher had not accepted the poor work, because it made the boy feel "that's the way he thought I really was." Unless and until re-lationship is established, teachers are unlikely to see boys as they really are—much less at their best. And as we have stressed, the invitation to relationship and the responsibility for its ongoing management largely falls—by default—to the teacher.

CHAPTER TEN

When Teachers Cannot Relate

IN CONTRAST TO THE boys' narratives described in the preceding chapter, the teacher accounts in our study *did* express concern about their responsibility for relational failure as well as considerable regret when a working relationship could not be achieved. In fact, both in survey responses and in workshops, teachers' accounts of these breakdowns were poignant and sometimes quite painful to read and hear. Teachers characterized their relational impasses as times of personal disappointment, hurt, or anger.

Like the boys, though, teachers typically absolved themselves from blame in these accounts, many of which were nonetheless rendered with a touching depth of feeling. Some of the most wrenching narratives recounted the teacher's experience of failing to reach a student years earlier. Understandably, if not helpfully, teachers often tried to distance themselves from students with whom they failed to relate. Most commonly, they attributed the failure of their relational efforts to boys' unreachability, brought about by personal shortcomings, family circumstances, psychological problems, or, in some cases, larger cultural forces. Whether or not these extramural causes were actually at work in boys' resistance, teachers' determining that a student was unreachable served to close off the relationship and with it the possibility of positive transformation.

Sometimes teachers faulted a boy's character, attributing relational failure to the boy's refusal to maintain a sufficient work ethic. These stories stood in sharp contrast to those in positive accounts in which a teacher's high standards, willingness to help, and commanding presence dissolved prior resistance to engagement and effort. In addition to their tendency to psychologize and even pathologize boys with whom they were unable to relate, some teachers also attributed boys' unreachability to larger social forces: prevailing gender attitudes, ethnicity, or social class. While it is widely acknowledged that racially or economically marginalized boys can pose special scholastic and relational challenges, Pedro Noguera of the Metropolitan Center for Urban Education at New York University has cautioned that "the research never suggested that poor children are incapable of learning." In fact, in schools that record measurably better achievement on the part of disadvantaged boys, including boys of color, "strong, positive relationships between students and teachers are critical ingredients," a finding confirmed emphatically in the stories collected for this study.[1]

Our study documents the positive impact of teachers who persevere with boys whose social circumstances bear negatively on their inclination to engage in assigned schoolwork. Again, teachers, like their students, carry their relational histories with them into the classroom. They too are subject to unexamined, reflexive responses to challenges posed by the students in their charge. Teachers' responsibility to serve as relationship managers, however, requires a capacity for reflection and self-awareness, a willingness to reassess present practice and to improvise—qualities often absent in teachers' stories of failed attempts to connect. Both the positive and negative teacher narratives tended to begin with relational challenges to be overcome—boys whose resistance required special attention and a willingness to adjust present practice. Relationally successful teachers reported positive transformations with boys beset by the same—or worse—circumstances as those bearing on boys determined to be unreachable in the accounts of failed relationship.

The following narrative, composed by an American teacher of middle school boys, reveals something of the depth and range of measures taken by teachers determined to build a productive relationship in the face of situational obstacles:

I started working with [this boy] as his sixth-grade drama teacher. While he was a talented actor, his behavior was difficult. He was oppositional, loud, and little bizarre at times. He screamed at classmates whenever anything went awry. Most surprising was that my dominating physical presence and booming voice did little to quell his outbursts. In fact, it fueled them. I managed to get through the trimester by treating [the student] with kid gloves and avoiding any confrontation. The following fall, I was momentarily dismayed when I saw [his] name on the roster of my seventh-grade English and social studies course. I knew I couldn't go through the year in a state of uneasy truce with him. I needed to reach him somehow. [The boy] started his seventh-grade year on probation for threatening a classmate [the] previous spring. He wanted to stay at our school and had undergone group therapy over the summer. He was motivated to do well, but he still repeatedly caused trouble in and out of the classroom. [He] dressed all in black. He wrote angry stories of death and destruction. He glared menacingly at anyone who crossed him in the slightest and he seemed paranoid about being bullied. I doubted that [he] would make it through the year. Gradually [he] began to trust me. This started with tearful conversations about wanting to be a good kid and wanting to make friends. He was quite articulate about his learning styles and about the demons in his head. Perhaps the first step to integrating him with his peers was when he spoke openly about his diagnosis of Obsessive Compulsive Disorder, and how hard it was for him to deal with something as seemingly simple as going to bed. [He] was touched when one of the more popular boys in the class responded "that must be so tough to live with." The warm response by the class as a whole helped [him] hope that he could eventually make a friend. Academically a breakthrough came after I read *Boy Writers* by Ralph Fletcher, and realized that [the boy's] violence-laced stories were actually beautifully crafted. He started to read his work out loud to his classmates, and I soon found out that he wrote extensively on his own at home. His classmates loved his stories, and he soon had a followership. [He] then started to lead adventure reenactments of some of his action stories during recess. [Spies] and villains and cops stalked each other throughout the halls. It was a risk to let the lid off his creativity, but [the student] soon blossomed. He stopped dressing all in black, so people stopped calling him a "Goth." What is the opposite of a vicious circle? [He] later went on to make a terrific film of a research project our class was undertaking, and he presented his beautifully edited movie to the school on the same stage that he had battled me [on] the year before.

In instances like this one, we were able to see how much a teacher's *interpretation* of the boy's condition affected the relationship's trajectory. Interpretations and predictions made on the basis of what teachers initially perceive in a boys' performance and outward manner, though influential, can be unreliable. Negative or pessimistic interpretations arise most often when teachers feel under particular stresses, stresses that might challenge their sense of professional competence and general self-worth. Whatever their situational cause, gloomy, pessimistic interpretations establish what Nakkula and Ravitch call a "projective arc" that limits the positive remedial responses teachers might make.[2]

Such limitations may have been at work in this candid narrative composed by a South African teacher after assessing a difficult boy's "challenges at home":

A reason for being unable to establish a decent relationship with [this student] is that, quite frankly, the prospect was too exhausting—we don't have much common ground [and] I couldn't detect any desire on his part to connect, and so it would have been a contrived relationship, which carries no weight in terms of truly reaching a person's heart. I knew that he was continuing to struggle with growing family challenges at home, but he wore a poker face by day. It was very difficult to tell when anything was bothering him. One thing remained clear, and that was that the academic challenges of school provided little joy for him. As I reflect on [him], I wonder what I might have done differently. He was clearly a kid who needed help, but he didn't want it. He was interested in being cool [and] playing sports, and I think most importantly, he wanted to come across as a strong young man [so] asking for help, or accepting it, must have felt like a sign of weakness. This was by far for me the biggest obstacle—one which I was unable to overcome. He certainly has solid potential, but getting him to believe in himself [is] key. I guess I wasn't the right person to do that, but I am confident that he will find someone else who can. I have to admit by his junior year I found I just didn't want to make the effort anymore. He constantly scowled at me and others, treated his peers with disrespect, and showed contempt for almost everything. This is a terrible thing for a teacher/coach to admit, but I gave up. So I'm sure he sensed my dislike for him. I justified this by saying he showed no respect toward me and clearly disliked me. I felt I had really tried with him during his first two years. He had a reputation in the lower school for being a bit petulant and volatile and I felt we had a decent relationship his freshman year. And then I couldn't get over my own frustration with him and I'm sure he fed off of that. When he graduated I felt a sense of relief and regret. He was difficult to deal with, but I felt I had not done enough to reach him. He graduated angry at me.

The sense of nagging regret that lingered after failing to meet this boy's challenges was a recurring theme in teachers' negative relationship narratives. Very frequently teachers recalled with haunting detail instances of failed relationships that had occurred years or even decades earlier.

Since teachers necessarily stand as authority figures to their students, it is not surprising that students may to some extent project parent-related feelings onto them. Teachers who are unaware of these projections and who take them personally may defend themselves from the unpleasantness by distancing themselves, disconnecting, or refusing relationship. Or, as in this South African teacher's account, they may recognize the underlying parental conflict but determine that resolving it is beyond their professional reach:

> [This student] was a very troublesome child with a complete lack of respect for authority—if anything, he seemed to thrive on "bucking the system." Upon further investigation, I found that he had a terrible relationship with his father—to the point where [the father] had disowned him—and it was this that led to his resistance in the classroom. Any effort to discipline him would elicit the response he would give to his own parents. It was unfortunate that no middle ground could be found with regards to [the boy's] behaviour and I am not sure how much longer he will survive at our school.

Without discounting the severity of some boys' struggles with their families, once a teacher interprets the situation as offering no room for relational negotiation, further effort and improvisation become unlikely. Reading these accounts of negative relationships, we were often struck by the severity of the stresses boys carry with them to school and the inevitable challenges such boys posed for their teachers. But we were also struck by teachers' hopes to succeed with each and every boy, evident both in their efforts to help and in the profound regret they express when they fail.

Teachers' understanding of boys' family circumstances was often a critical factor in both relational success and failure. In their stories of successful relationships, many teachers gratefully acknowledged the parental cooperation and resulting sense of partnership they experienced as they worked to meet boys' scholastic and personal needs. In the unsuccessful accounts, by contrast, teachers described being at cross-purposes with parents they felt were making unreasonable demands, were unsupportive of the teacher's efforts to help, or failed to provide sufficient nurture or supervision to enable the boy to function effectively in school.

This American teacher of Spanish, like many of her colleagues internationally, expressed exasperation with parents who were quick to assign blame for boys' problems to teachers' shortcomings, but disinclined to see their son's contribution to the problem:

> The relationship that did not succeed was with a student who was in a second-year Spanish class three years ago. He left school in the middle of the fall of his sophomore year and returned to his public high school. He was a weak student and did not put forth much effort. For me the main obstacle to not having him succeed were his parents. As soon as he received a low grade, one or both of them called and went over the test and questioned why points were taken off. Not once did they question their son's effort. This not only occurred in my class, but in other classes and on the football field. The parents constantly questioned the teacher's tests, attitudes, and for coaches the playing time for their son. The parents told me more than once that the faculty was out to get their son and break him. It was almost an impossible task to try to reach this young man, as he would say that he needed to speak to his parents before he could respond to others or to me. When his parents decided to take him out of the school, many of us felt relieved. But I did worry that now [that] he was even closer to home in his public school he would never learn to be independent nor cope with any setbacks on his own.

The following narrative expresses the frustration teachers often feel when their ability to work with boys is undercut by a parent. The British teacher here also reveals an unmistakable certainty that his analysis of the boy's circumstances is correct and that no further measures on his or the school's part were appropriate; like so many of the negative relational accounts, this one expresses regret that the boy was not reachable, but little doubt as to the cause.

A relationship was established with a particular student upon [his] arrival into the school as a year-eight pupil through being placed into my tutor group. The student in question was a self-conscious individual with a very poor home/family background. The relationship had evolved over the eighteen months that the student was in my tutor group from year eight to nine. As a popular young man, the student started his school career well with support from his foster parents at home and my relationship with him was very positive. Toward the end of year eight the student moved back in with his mother, which began a downward spiral. His characteristics increasingly advocated a lack of enthusiasm for school and his attendance began to decline rapidly. His mother and grandparents were very supportive but failed to deal with appropriate discipline at home, which prevented his attending school. At school, many special measures were put in place and taken into consideration. The boy in question was a talented footballer, and if he completed a period in school he was allowed to participate in sporting fixtures. The student was also allowed to drop certain subjects, and a reduced timetable was produced for him to help him achieve in the subjects he enjoyed and needed for further career ideas. Study periods were incorporated into his timetable and I implemented a number of one-to-one sessions and interviews. Unfortunately, by the spring term in year nine the student had become a nonattender. After daily contact from his mother and grandmother, informing us they could not get him to come into school, a number of home visits were made by myself, his head of year, and [the] deputy head. The visits showed a short-term improvement, but very quickly old habits had returned. In the meantime, support for the mother was put in place (family support worker) and the matter continued to remain the same. Eventually the boy began home tutoring and has not attended school since. It is a shame that a boy who had a good start at the school, with so much potential, pressed the self-destruct button and lost all of the opportunities available to him.

A perceived lack of motivation and effort from underperforming boys frustrated many of the teachers who recounted failed relationships. These narratives often assumed that the extra effort expended by teachers to form a productive relationship with an underperforming boy should be earned. This veteran American teacher, despite repeated attempts to engage a resistant underperformer, contends that without the student's determination to try and to "care," there can be no forward progress. Moreover, as this story illustrates, such refusals from boys can elicit a "sense of betrayal" in their teachers.

> Though this school year is only half done, I have two students who are not working anywhere near their potential. I have to ask myself if there is a better way to approach them, a better way to teach them the material. I have to ask myself if it is because they feel that I don't care about them, have not connected with them. The second student is where my serious frustration lies. This student came to our school from a public school, and has a lot of time management and "how to study" issues. This student has come to our school with very high athletic prospects. In academics (or at least in my class), though, he projects an attitude of not wanting to bother with the learning. During the first semester, I went way beyond trying to reach this young man. I offered to help him before school, allowed him to redo assignments, retake quizzes and tests, and finish assignments very late. In class, I tried to be sensitive to calling on him and putting him on the spot. Before and after class, I talked to him to try to get a feel for what he thought he could get finished. Though at times, I felt that we were making some progress, overall, there was never a sense of being connected. I did not have a sense that he cared about doing well in my class [and] unfortunately, I have not seen appreciable effort in my class. Though I want to be fair with him, I feel a personal sense of betrayal. To succeed as a fine man as well as a fine athlete, one also needs to be willing to buy into all that involves, on and off the court.

It is perhaps instructive that two distinctive features of the negative relational accounts were often linked: (1) the depth of feeling that teachers expressed at "losing" a boy, even years after the event, and (2) the retained conviction that, whether willed or circumstantial, the fault lay entirely with the boy or his circumstances. Even when, as in the following account from an American teacher and coach, there is a germ of self-questioning ("I probably did not have the skills to handle him"), the accounts of relational failure usually find against the boy and for the approaches adopted by the teacher and the school.

> Early in my career, I was the teacher and advisor of a boy who was asked to leave the school at the end of the year. I feel as though I never got through to this student, no matter what I tried. Looking back, I probably didn't have the skills to handle him, and he needed someone who could be much more effective. The boy signed up for my class, woodworking, so it was natural that he would be in my advisory. He was a big guy and had a reputation of not pushing himself very hard. He was a sophomore trying out for varsity football (I was one of the assistant coaches) and the prospect was good. In our initial meeting I told him that there were going to be a lot of demands on him in the upper school and that the stakes were higher. The boy seemed optimistic and hopeful for the year. Several weeks into school, he realized that he wasn't making the impact in football that he had hoped. Other coaches mentioned to me that he had the size, but he wasn't doing much with it. At the same time, school started to get harder for him. The boy's work in my class was being poorly done. He was rushing through things and complaining to other students that he didn't like the work. His other teachers were notifying me about his lack of effort in their classes. [When I tried] to talk to him about woodworking, the conversation would soon spill into other problems he was having. Most of what I was trying to relate was that his effort needed to improve. The more I checked in on him, the more he seemed to dig in his heels. Before the first semester ended, the boy and I met with the director of the upper school to try to turn him around. By the end of the year, he had several Ds on his report card, had been cited for a major cheating violation, and had used up much of his goodwill with other faculty members. I remember when the faculty voted that he not return, and I thought it was the right decision.

In addition to citing boys' unwillingness to work and to try, other faculty narratives attributed relational failure to factors beyond teachers' pedagogical reach—most typically boys' limited ability or prior learning deficits. While such attributions served to absolve the narrating teacher of blame, the resulting failure of the boy to achieve and for boy and teacher to connect carried a residue of emotional frustration, as conveyed in this narrative from an American mathematics teacher.

I still ponder if there was something more that I should have done to help this boy. He was a kind boy with an odd sense of humor. He was a student in my homeroom class who was working far below grade level, struggling in English, mathematics, and geography. He had difficulty understanding the material in most lessons. I often taught the lesson to the class and then sat with this boy to offer him additional help; he learned best one-on-one. Writing was particularly challenging for him due to poor handwriting and difficulty expressing himself. He was always the last student to complete each task. He also struggled in mathematics. The boy did not know his basic math facts and learning new concepts did not come easy to him. During the first quarter, I shared with the boy's parents that he was working below grade level but that I would work with him to help him improve. The parents told me that it was taking their son hours to complete his homework each night. The boy appeared very sullen in class. The mother reported that he remarked that he hated his life. Though he worked steadily during class time, the boy often ended the day with incomplete assignments. I began making arrangements for him to arrive early or stay after school to complete his work. As the school year progressed, the boy continued to need extra time to complete most assignments. He never quite learned his multiplication facts, and he did poorly in geography as well. At the close of the year, the boy was still having difficulty in every subject area. He never quite learned his basic math facts, and writing remained a chore for him. Each Friday, the boy remained after school to complete assignments that he was unable to finish in class. Though he was ultimately able to complete all of his tasks given the extra time, this student never achieved grade-level performance. Additionally, his demeanor remained unhappy.

Sometimes the resistance boys offer teachers cannot be assigned neatly to known learning difficulties, troubled domestic circumstances, or psychological problems. Sometimes teachers experience what appears to be a simple refusal, as this American teacher related, revealing a gap that can open between a teacher's efforts and a boy's engagement when there is little relationship:

> This boy, a junior, was in my precalculus class. This course is a requirement for graduation. This boy did not take notes in my class; did not turn in his homework assignments; and did not answer any questions on the quizzes. He started putting his head down on the desk, which I did not allow. He was told that if he slept in class, he would get a detention. Basically, he did nothing in precalculus. When I attempted to talk to him about his lack of progress in my class, his attitude was, "I'm here to play football." I spoke to the head of the upper school about the situation. She had a meeting with the boy, but this did not change his behavior. I asked him to come see me during study hall; he did not. I talked to his advisor and football coaches. They spoke to the boy; no change. I sent comments home at the mid-quarter and at the end of the quarter, describing his lack of work. I had no response from the parents. I told him that if he saw me during his free period, I would help him catch up in class, and that he could pass. He did not come to see me. After about the middle of the second quarter, I felt my hands were tied. The boy was too far behind in the material, and he made no effort to do any work. He failed for the year. With the threat of being dismissed [from] the school if he did not pass precalculus in summer school, he passed the course with no trouble. I was not the summer school teacher.

Teachers' relational narratives—both positive and negative—included many instances of difficulties relating to boys known or believed to be suffering from psychological distress. The positive narratives documented the pleasure and satisfaction teachers experienced when a productive working alliance was achieved, despite seeming barriers, and the boy's needs were met. The following accounts suggest some of the frustration teachers encounter when they find the challenges posed to be beyond their means of remediation.

A Canadian teacher determined that she "did not have the tools at her disposal" to help a boy who would at times present himself as "an unpredictable beast." Her difficulties in this instance were compounded by the fact that the boy's parents were resistant to counseling and her administrators were reluctant to address the obstacles the boy posed to classroom management.

> I can't even remember the child's name, but I'll never forget him. The family had just moved into the neighborhood and would be leaving at the end of the year. This boy was troubled and he was trouble in the classroom and in the yard. It was a third-grade split primary class with twenty-seven students and it was a busy place. It was an activity-based program so that the students could all work at their various levels. He seemed like a nice enough child, liked to do his work (at a below-average level), [and] was proud of everything he accomplished in class, but he had no sense of control or empathy. Every so often, something would come over him and he became an unpredictable beast. I was not equipped to deal with him and his outbursts. Often I would have to physically remove him from our circle or from a group of children sitting at an assembly. I was forced to send him to the office on many occasions, one of which was when he raised his pencil in the air and stabbed another child in the hand. The parents were called regularly, but they were not helpful when it came to their son's social problems. When it was suggested that the boy needed psycho-educational testing (the other parents were threatening to pull their children from the class, as they felt too much of my time was used for settling this boy down), the mother became fiercely protective and was adamant that she and her husband would not allow this. I tried to anticipate stressful situations to avoid the potential outbursts. I asked him to sit next to me in circles

so that I could be close enough to stop him from confronting another child. I kept him very busy with appropriate activities and gave him lots of praise for acceptable behavior. Nonetheless he continued to be disruptive and difficult, and he never reached the point where he respected me enough to continuously behave properly toward his classmates. I still wonder whatever happened to that boy.

Some boys may, at least for a time, be lost to those seeking to reach and teach them, and while conscientious teachers may forever wonder "what if" some alternative, untried approach might have created a working relationship, it is impossible to know. This dedicated and long-serving Canadian teacher, like many of her colleagues, was able to conclude nothing further in her account of a failed relationship than that she had done everything thing she could:

> This boy was one of the most difficult students I have ever worked with. I used every engagement technique that I have accumulated in my thirty years of being in education. I would spend one-to-one time talking with him, supervising and monitoring him, organizing him to no avail. He was reclusive, evasive, and extremely disengaged with the world. His self-esteem was almost nonexistent. His family situation placed enormous pressure on him to succeed, but this only distanced him further from school and success. Unfortunately, I was caught between demands of his parents and the needs of this lost boy. I eventually had to seek further support from our social worker and insist that the family seek further outside support. He eventually stopped coming to school. I wanted to believe that I could assist him, but the issue was much larger than I knew about. I knew that I had to move on to help others. He sought psychiatric help and eventually enrolled in an alternative school. I have heard that he is taking part-time university courses.

While teachers were sometimes not beyond admitting misjudgment and outright mistakes, there was also evidence in narratives, such as this one from an American track coach, that while he may have made a particular misstep or two in response to a problematic boy, in the final analysis he was probably in the right.

> My work with this next student may ultimately evince some of the same long-term payoffs as my work with the first one, but in the short term the disappointments were more evident. This boy's main challenge was that his low self-esteem demanded constant attention; his valuing of the more superficial aspects of the sport (varsity letter status, running in a varsity race) stemmed in large part from his insecurity. To run in a varsity race meant validation. To earn a varsity letter brought him a status that he craved in so many ways but found difficult to gain in almost all areas of his life. On one occasion, at the conclusion of a cross-country season, I left him off of the varsity letter list. I assumed I had done the right thing; varsity letters at the time were earned by those running varsity races, and since he had not run in one that year he would get a junior varsity letter instead. The night after our seasonal sports assembly where the letters are announced, I received a phone call from his parents, who informed me that their son was distraught over not earning a letter. I explained the protocol to them and offered to come over right then to comfort the boy. When I arrived and began speaking with him, he pointed out that he had run in a varsity race mid-season. Upon reflection, I realized I was wrong and that he should have earned a varsity letter. The next day, when I checked my records, I spoke with the boy, awarded him the letter, and then called the parents and apologized. "An honest mistake made by an honest man," or something along those lines, was the gracious response by the father. One year later, when confronted with the challenge of whom to place in the varsity championship race, I entered a sophomore who had beaten this boy on several occasions leading up to that race, and placed the boy in the junior varsity race. Once again, he was devastated. The comment from his mother this time was that "you talk about winning not being the most important thing, but it's clear in your actions that it is." I had failed to connect with the boy with regard to the sport's most important meaning. Whether the greatest

obstacle was his low self-esteem, which needed a more measurable nourishing than the sport's more esoteric, to him, meaning or the emphasis placed by his parents on those more surface-level rewards was hard for me to discern.

A number of gender-related assumptions came to bear on how both boys and teachers assessed their relationships. Some female teachers attributed boys' lack of receptivity to relationship to their inability to relate to women generally, as suggested by this Australian teacher:

> A dismissive, misogynistic student could not cope with the prospect of having a female teacher. He spent two years making snide remarks, and apparently dismissing anything that I had to say. I tried hard to give him additional information—and could never convince him that what I had to say was valid. All I managed to do was ensure an excellent result for him—but the relationship remained fractured.

While we observed many female teachers extending the positive gestures discussed in earlier chapters to build successful relationships, a number of them sensed that boys' opposition was sometimes specifically directed to them as women. This American biology teacher reports taking pains to assure a persistently resistant boy that she was fully a "human being," but beyond speculating that the boy may have experienced a prior bad experience with a woman in authority, she was unable to soften his resistance or form a satisfactory relationship with him:

> In contrast to the good relationships I have had with students, I think about this one boy. From day one, he was unwilling to see me as a human being. I was a teacher, yes, but never a person to him. Although most of my students would say that I am knowledgeable and caring, I am not sure that he would ever say this. He would oppose everything that I would say or suggest to him. It could be a test grade or a homework grade. It really didn't matter. Despite my best efforts to get to know him, he did not let me in. I lived at the

school in an all-girls dorm so knew most of the students at the small school. I gave my personal life/time/energy to the students every day of the week. Because of our close quarters, my life was very inter-twined with the students. Although my dorm was a girl's dorm, the boys were always around. This boy was too. He actually dated one of the girls in my dorm. I tried to get to know him outside of the biol-ogy classroom, but it didn't matter. His body language told me that he had no interest in getting to know me as a person. My now ex-husband was his dorm parent. We both tried to figure out what had happened. I can only imagine that it wasn't really me but a relation-ship with a female that was not positive in his life. I tried to keep this boy after school to give him extra help, but he was so uncomfortable in my room that I let him go. To this day, I have wondered what else I could have done to help this young man. I did find out that only with the males on campus did he have a good relationship. I spoke to the school psychologist to get some insight—even he was stumped. It is funny, I have made such positive connections to students—boys and girls—that it is the one or two students who don't go well who stay with me. Why is that?

Boys' stereotypic masculine reactions and attitudes were not re-stricted to their dealings with female teachers and could confound teaching relationships with males as well. A New Zealand phys-ics teacher and rugby coach found himself engaged in a "power struggle" with a popular but resistant boy. As lines were drawn as to whether teacher or boy held more influence over the boy's "posse," the underlying mission of reaching and helping the boy was scuttled.

I have had a few relationships with students that have been less ef-fective. What follows is an account of a student where I really strug-gled to engage him for long periods of time during 2010. It was my first year teaching at this school and I was the new boy on the block. This boy (year-twelve student) was very much the "man about town." He was likely to be in the first XV and this, as a year twelve student, held some currency. I always felt that there was an uneasy, almost suspicious feeling toward me. He always gave me the impression that he knew more than me on a number of issues. I was teaching him Level 2 Physics in a big class and several of his classmates thought very highly of him, idolized him . . . I was enjoying teaching the class, but there was a posse around this boy that made behavior management more difficult. He was highly thought of by other staff throughout the school—he became a prefect during 2011 and likely first XV captain—and I think he felt like he could do what he liked in my class as no one would believe the "newbe" that he was anything less than fantastic in physics. This boy also knew, correctly as it turned out, that he could cruise through the year and be okay in the end. His examinations during the year were poor, but his NCEA assessments (both internal and external) were better than average. It was not what he was capable of and this was the basis for my reporting to parents and my conversations with him, but his results were reasonable nonetheless. It is important to note that this class, the boy himself, or the posse around him never turned into a circus, but there was often a feeling that it was "the boy versus the teacher" on some very basic issues such as time management, homework, completing tasks in class, and generally acceptable noise level in class. The posse would often look around to see what his reaction was to my instructions and get their cue from him. I needed to split up the posse. I did this most of the time and tried to spend some one-on-one time with each of the class to help them do better . . . I was always in amongst the groups physically and worked really hard to keep good established class routines. I spent time with the boy to help him with some issues he was having with the subject. I talked to him about the unhealthy relationship that was developing between him, his group of followers, and me. I explained that the trouble was, although he was going to be okay at the end of the year, many of his friends were going to struggle if their work didn't improve. I took an interest in his rugby, but I didn't believe he was anywhere near as good as others had told him he was for several years. I was the New Zealand Schools coach at the time and I really tried to help him on a basic issue that he was particularly bad at, but still he gave me the impression that he was a little above his station. I was really conscious never to take him on head to head, as this is what he really wanted and his group was looking for. I removed him from class twice—something that I generally never do.

While a reliable approach to dissolving boys' showy "macho" opposition eluded many of the writers of these narratives, this American teacher became painfully aware that taking the matter angrily into his own hands—literally—was emphatically not the answer:

This is a terrible story. When I was first teaching, I had this student . . . In class he was not interested in participating in the discussion; he was interested in disrupting it, and his technique always involved calling attention to himself. He told unwanted stories of his weekend, he made fun of other students, he made lewd comments, and he laughed at any awkwardness I showed. As a young teacher I didn't know many ways to try to break through. Early on I found out a full-frontal attack didn't work. When asked a direct question about why he behaved as he did, he never responded with the truth—only with sarcasm. When I tried to find a shred in an inappropriate story about his weekend and see if I could tease anything out that might make him interested in school, he was smart enough to trounce all over my efforts. Every time he returned from the dean or principal's office, he announced to the class that he got off scot-free, and when the dean told me that young man did not, I begin to wonder whether anyone in the school could change this boy, and by extension, whether anyone could help me at my work. The climax came during a last period of the day. Our school had students pick up attendance slips each period—we left them in the door and were not supposed to be disturbed. But also an announcement list was sometimes sent out. [The boy] burst into my class without knocking and shouted at the top of his voice that he had announcements to read. It was rude. It was in keeping. To be short, I carried him out of the room and told him never again. The headmaster came to see me late that afternoon to tell me the boy and his father [were] in his office. Only by the grace of God, the patience of the head and his belief in me, and the time this occurred (many years ago) did I keep my job.

The impact of gender was only one social pressure cited by teachers as limiting their relationships with boys. Boys who identified themselves as economically or culturally marginalized became for some teachers relationally unreachable. One American teacher and coach, while appreciating the special adjustments required of an African American boy from an urban neighborhood whose financially struggling family sought a higher quality, safer academic experience at an elite suburban school, reveals the relational missteps that can occur when teachers are unaware of their own racial assumptions and stereotypes.

> It is very difficult sometimes for an inner-city boy to make the incredible transition from a dysfunctional school system and an unstable, often dangerous neighborhood to a private school campus where a large percentage of students drive expensive new cars to school every day and talk about summer homes and trips abroad. This boy, who graduated twenty years ago, was a charming, smart, athletically gifted young boy of thirteen when he came to our school as a first former. He was so endearing and energetic that he made friends fast and earned the affection of all of his teachers and coaches as soon as his first year with us commenced. Over the next six years, however, I believe he learned how to play the game of feeding upon the natural inclination of a generally all-white, well-educated, and affluent school community. His charm often encouraged some of his mentors to look the other way when he passed in a paper late or transgressed a school rule. I believe that I, as his teacher and two-sport coach (cross-country running and track) fell into this trap, and I regret that I did not mentor him with more firmness. I also think that, at the time, a lack of presence of African American teachers and students on campus made this boy feel like an outsider who could be most valued by behaving like a comedian instead of being taken seriously for his clearly superior intelligence. I also blame this, in part, on a faculty [that] was all too willing to view him as a special

"project" through whom they could assuage their baggage of "white guilt" by bending over backward to accommodate his needs. While everyone had the best of intentions, we all succumbed to the notion that what this boy needed was the gift of unconditional acceptance and kindness rather than the gift of discipline and clear direction in life. Coming from a broken family, he attracted the goodwill of one of our nicest families, who offered to take him into their home. This boy was a teammate of two of their sons, so it seemed like a good idea. Unfortunately, things soon went downhill. He soon developed an air of entitlement and started to take advantage of his host family's generosity. One Saturday night, while the parents were away, the boy took the keys to a family car and totaled it in an accident while visiting friends from his old neighborhood. Luckily, he was not hurt. Of course, this was it for his host parents, and he was asked to leave the house for good. While he did eventually graduate and went on to a prestigious local university, he had some run-ins with the law before he finally settled down and straightened out his life, by and large. While we and other independent schools have done a much better job of diversifying our student bodies more effectively, there still remains the need to understand when good intentions and kindness become a kind of unintended patronization—something that can be quite damaging at times.

Cultural stereotypes and projections can limit even well-intentioned teachers as they attempt to mitigate class- and race-based pressures on the boys in their charge. This American teacher, for example, wrote of feeling "manipulated" because of his willingness to accommodate a student who "did not have many of the resources that the other students did":

This boy was older than all of the other kids in class. He came from a disadvantaged household and didn't have many, if [any], of the resources that most of the others students had. He entered seventh grade as a new student while the rest of the class already knew each other. This kid was bright, and I was aware of this based on his performance in other classes; however, he had a sassy attitude in my class. I offered extra help [to] him. I was available early morning, during lunch hour, and after school. I tried to understand his situation and even sympathize with it. I made lesson plans targeting his interest and gave praise whenever he participated in class. He had never taken a foreign language before. He was not interested in Spanish. He wanted to focus on disrupting the class. There was a point when I felt that he knew I was willing to go above and beyond to reach him and he manipulated many situations. He was a resistant, noncooperative student. I felt like I was never able to reach him, but [to] this day I am not sure I could have [gotten] him to work and build a teacher-student relationship with him.

An Australian teacher related the frustration she experienced as a result of being assigned to teach indigenous boys at levels beyond what she believed they could possibly master. Her dedicated efforts to form relationships with such boys, while not altogether futile, were severely limited by the school's untenable commitment to predetermined standards.

The biggest obstacle I have faced when trying to establish a good learning relationship with a boy has been the level of academic achievement required for success. My school offers scholarships to indigenous students, who frequently arrive with limited academic skills at the middle of senior secondary end of their education. It is very hard to close the gap for these boys, as time is short and the standard is so high that their skills fall short. These boys quickly become dispirited and are keen to leave the school. I am convinced that a more flexible curriculum with more hands-on subjects would have made a difference to their achievement hopes. I tried to focus on establishing a good emotional relationship with the students; however, this frequently does not compensate for the lack of achievement they feel academically and they then give up and return home. A different curriculum and intensive cultural/educational support plus an initial long-term orientation program prior to school entry would certainly have enhanced these students' chance of success. We need to look at what they can offer the school community rather than just what we can give them if they are to feel successful.

Taken together, as unhappy and sometimes tragic as they are, these accounts of failed relationship reveal patterns that point the way to improved practice. In both their positive and negative narratives, teachers reported taking special measures to address the problems and needs of resistant boys, but the positive accounts documented success with boys whose patterns of resistance and unsatisfactory performance were often indistinguishable from those featured in the negative narratives. The successful accounts included features that might have improved the outcome of the unsuccessful ones. For example, although both positive and negative accounts reveal teachers who were willing to *attempt* relationship, the successful narratives indicated an openness to continuous reassessment less apparent in the negative narratives. Whatever theory or analytic construct was guiding teachers in the successful accounts, when an approach did not seem to work, the teachers were willing to reconsider assumptions and improvise new approaches. In the negative accounts, by contrast, when favored remedial approaches failed to achieve intended results, there was a tendency to determine that a boy was beyond the teacher's—or perhaps any teacher's—capacity to reach and to help. In such instances, the teacher's allegiance to his or her viewpoint precluded further attempts to achieve relationship.

In both positive and negative accounts, boys often presented provocative opposition and resistance in class and were defiant about changing those behaviors when confronted. Unlike teachers who insisted that boys themselves must first "buy in" to the partnership with respect and effort, teachers who succeeded in dissolving resistance and hostility assumed the responsibility of relationship manager. Whether prompted by experience or learned theory, such teachers did not expect students to assume mutual responsibility for a working alliance, and especially not when the boy was under some duress. Teachers as relationship managers were able to convey to resistant boys that they, the teachers, (1) were effectively in charge, (2) were positively concerned about the boys despite their poor performance or troublesome behavior, and (3) were confident that better work and better behavior were possible—even when no such work or behavior was yet evident.

While by no means suggesting that the challenges posed by boys beset by racial and other forms of social marginalization are easily met, we are encouraged by the relational successes reported by New Zealand teachers in their relationships with Maori boys, Australian teachers with Aboriginal boys, British and Canadian teachers with immigrant boys from countries around the world, and American teachers with boys of Latin or African American heritage. Whatever strategies are abandoned and adopted along the way, teachers committed to relational connection clearly *do succeed* in overcoming culturally imposed barriers to educational opportunity.

None of the foregoing should be taken to imply that the teachers narrating relational breakdown and failure were simply unskilled and mistaken and could have done better. Many teachers whose negative relational narratives are cited herein expended admirable extra effort to reach difficult boys who may well have been beyond their or their school's capacity to reach and help. Those points established, however, it is still promising to consider how unproductive relationships might be transformed to productive ones by teachers' willingness to step back and reassess (1) the priority and role of relationship in boys' scholastic success, and (2) how one's disposition to assign cause to boys' psychological, social, and other circumstantial factors might prevent relational connections that could otherwise enable boys to succeed.

CHAPTER ELEVEN

■ ■ ■

Becoming a
Relational School

ESTABLISHING RELATIONAL teaching and learning as a governing feature of school life requires nothing less than a paradigm shift as to what constitutes good schooling. School leaders' mere appreciation of teachers who appear to relate especially well to students will not suffice to create a more productive relational climate in the school. That kind of transformation will occur only when school leaders embrace the conviction that relationship does not merely enhance scholastic experience; it is the very *medium* through which students' engagement, effort, and ultimate mastery are realized.

Establishing the primacy of relationship in schools also invites a frank reckoning with alternate approaches to school reform that are demonstrably not working. Foremost among these are "high control" professional development approaches calling for tighter supervision and more frequent assessments of teachers' performance and credentials. School leaders who conflate teacher quality with their students' measurable performance on standardized tests pose special obstacles to positive relationship building. Teachers are most likely to reflect openly on their practice and to thrive professionally when, as Ted Purinton has suggested, they are regarded as "knowledge workers," whose skills grow in peer exchanges of ideas, concepts, and information. Under the right conditions, teachers as knowledge workers, as opposed to testing coaches, are open to challenging questions about the methods, substance, and purpose of their work with both colleagues and students. Such teachers attain mastery of the subjects and of their pedagogy through professional collaboration, not administrative fiat.[1]

Anthony Bryk and Barbara Schneider show in their study of the Chicago School Reform Act that "relational trust" distinguishes successful from less successful schools and that schools build relational capacity in an overall climate characterized by interpersonal respect, professional competence, and personal integrity. In a recent Gallup-Healthways Well-Being Index, teachers rated satisfaction with their occupational lives higher than any other group besides physicians. Though indicating *more day-to-day stress*, teachers also registered *more positive experiences*—including daily laughter—than any other group. While it might be assumed that such a highly satisfied work force would bode well for successful relationship making with students, the teachers polled also indicated ways in which they felt constrained from doing their professional best. In response to the prompt, "My supervisor creates an environment that is trusting and open," teachers ranked last among the field of occupations.[2]

The relational climate of schools at all levels bears directly on both teachers' inclination and ability to form productive relationships with individual students. Eleanor Drago-Severson, who has studied teachers' professional development, concluded that schools that promote teachers' continuing education are more likely to report success with student achievement: "Adult growth is directly and positively linked to increasing the academic achievement of children." Teachers invest themselves fully in their work with students when they are *supervised relationally*: guided by department chairs, curriculum specialists, and other administrators who convey trust, inspiration, and encouragement. Drago-Severson recommends a professional development approach characterized by observant peer relationships in which teacher performance can be assessed in mutually supportive ways: "I noted that when teachers, myself included, felt *well held* in a psychological sense—listened to, heard, and cared about by the administration—it seemed to have a direct and positive effect on the children."[3]

Teachers are likely to feel "well held" and thus inclined to invest themselves relationally with students when they share a school-wide consensus that relationship is foundational to school process at every level. Relational trust depends upon each person in the school—teacher, supervisor, manager—treating others in a manner consistent with professional expectations. Establishing this kind of relational climate, Bryk and Schneider concluded, is "the core resource" for overall school improvement. While it is encouraging that there is a growing consensus among educational theorists about the primacy of relationship in teaching and learning, there is at present no such consensus brewing among the general public, although public frustration with underperforming schools continues to escalate.

An April 12, 2013, *New York Times* editorial entitled "Teachers: Will We Ever Learn?" noted grimly that in the thirty years since the federally commissioned study, *A Nation at Risk*, documented the "rising tide of mediocrity" that had come to characterize American public education, students' measurable progress has generally *declined*—despite billions of dollars invested in new programs to establish statewide standardized testing, a proliferation of alternate charter schools, new teacher certification programs, increasing reliance on test-based "accountability," and the most ambitiously financed federal education programs in the nation's history, No Child Left Behind and Race to the Top. The striking lack of success of these structural reforms lends some urgency to look elsewhere for the factors that bear on improved learning and better schools.[4]

The successful relationships narrated by teachers in our study were broadly characterized by two qualities: (1) a willingness to be flexible and to improvise alternate approaches, and (2) a capacity to step back and reflect on what was working and not working in their relational efforts. Accepting their role as relationship manager, teachers persisted even when faced with what looked to them like repeated failure. These habits of improvisation and reflection are most likely to emerge in a school culture that explicitly values them and provides regular professional development opportunities for faculty to share their relational successes and challenges with their colleagues. These opportunities require, above all, that relational strains be viewed as occasions for professional growth rather than administrative judgment or more punitive sanctions.

Achieving relationally successful schools also requires discarding the widely held but unexamined assumption that relational effectiveness is beyond the personal range of certain faculty "types." The notion that relational effectiveness is an unevenly distributed "gift" and not susceptible to development was emphatically belied by the participating teachers in our study. Nearly all the accounts of relational success began with a relational problem that was ultimately overcome, often by a significant adjustment in the narrating teacher's practice. Teachers in these stories related overcoming what they thought were certain obstacles to getting to know and getting to work with boys they initially believed were "not their type." By contrast, teachers' accounts of relational failure were characterized by certainties that extramural factors bearing on students' lives or prior learning deficits made productive relationship impossible—even though the positive relational accounts addressed and reversed identical concerns. Again, one of the strongest findings of this study was that relationship building is a *developable* capacity.

To underscore the structural shifts required to elevate the relational dimension to a primary position within school curricula, we offer the following concrete suggestions for schools, for teachers, and for boys themselves.

STRATEGIES FOR SCHOOLS

Realistically, the creation of relationally effective schools will require a series of practical steps that embed the primacy of relationship making in school routines and structures. Many schools nod rhetorically in this direction but do little substantively to support faculty practices that would generate relational teaching.

The practical work of establishing the primacy of relationship begins with schools' governing boards and administrative leaders adopting mission statements acknowledging the foundational place of relationship in teaching and learning. This relational commitment should be clearly communicated to all school constituents, including parents and graduates, and built into the job descriptions and practical expectations for teachers, coaches, and other staff. Professional evaluation systems should include the relational dimension as well as the pedagogical and should specify supportive remedial practices for relationally struggling teachers.

Adequate professional development time—a precious and scarce commodity in schools—should be allocated for all faculty to assess relational progress and its obstacles, activities that should themselves be relational, allowing ample opportunity for peer exchanges and critical friend partnerships. There must also be continuing assessment of schools' structural variables that bear on relational potential, including class sizes, teachers' course loads and student loads, daily schedules, support and assessment of teachers from early to late career, and the creation of assessments and reports to families indicating relational, and not just scholastic, progress.

As suggested already, an essential feature of relational teaching is teachers' capacity for the *continuous reassessment* of their relational approaches. Teachers open to this kind of self-assessment should be fortified by the knowledge that every teacher, novice or master, experiences periodic relational snags and frustrations with students. In the right professional climate, teachers experiencing those challenges will find ready support and guidance from peers who have contended with similar problems. Colleagues, particularly those who have worked with the problematic student in different settings, are apt to be especially helpful in pointing out underlying factors in a student's resistance, including aversive prior scholastic experience, difficult domestic circumstances, and setbacks in a student's out-of-school pursuits. In sum, school leaders should work to create a scholastic community where the shared goal of relationship making provides occasions for positive collaboration among teachers and administrators.[5]

In practical terms, a shift from blame to support for teachers attempting to forge effective working alliances with highly resistant boys must be built into a supervisor's day-to-day management practice. Given how commonly boys demonstrate relational resistance, it is critical that teachers acknowledge their struggles with students' behavior without reverting to strategies of self-defense. Relationally committed supervisors can correct this tendency by establishing a climate of emotional safety among their colleagues, a climate in which teachers are comfortable confiding their unsuccessful efforts to reach students.[6]

For the past quarter-century, numerous educators and pundits have argued strenuously that the deprivations imposed by poverty and racial marginalization are the cause of scholastic failure in the United States, and that attempts to look elsewhere only prolong the problem. In our own research and as described herein, teachers struggling with a particular boy may seize upon these stressful circumstances as a way to cope with their own frustration or fears of failure. While race and poverty did indeed bear on the relational challenges facing teachers, many nonetheless reported gratifying—if not always immediate—success with such students, suggesting how even seemingly intractable student problems can be resolved through the creation of productive relationship.

Finally, it would be disingenuous and unhelpful to suggest to practicing teachers that a positive, productive relationship is possible in every instance. Extramural circumstances and constraints on necessary resources and time can pose insurmountable obstacles to even the best-intentioned, relationally deft teachers. Nevertheless, relationally committed teachers can take heart in our finding that, with sufficient willingness to reassess approaches over time—whether weeks, months, whole school terms, years—they can achieve remarkable transformation with the most seemingly intractable students. Whether or not schools can achieve productive relationship with every child enrolled, they are likely to experience gratifying transformations if that is their goal.

STRATEGIES FOR TEACHERS

As we have documented in the preceding chapters, there are multiple pathways to productive relationship, and such relationships are achieved by a broad range of personal types. It is instructive, however, to remember that both boys and teachers attributed relational success to a number of specific relational gestures, including:

- Being alert to and reaching out to meet individual students' needs
- Acknowledging and expressing interest in boys' special interests and talents
- Disclosing, where appropriate, teachers' own special interests and experiences
- Accommodating, within practical limits, a measure of opposition
- Admitting fault when appropriate, revealing vulnerability

The appreciation boys express for the relational gestures of their teachers is embedded in their larger assumption that teachers are supposed to be (1) masters of their subjects and masterful in conveying the material to them, and (2) interested in them and their progress. When either of these conditions is perceived to be unmet, the working alliance can break down. The expected mastery and personal interest on the part of their teachers is confirmed for the boys in classes where clear behavioral and scholastic expectations are established, as well as an assurance that students, with needed help, will meet those expectations. Boys across school types and national cultures also respond positively to teachers able to create a classroom atmosphere characterized by a sense of fairness and mutual respect—settings in which they feel emotionally safe. Boys are also warmly appreciative of such elementary gestures as teachers addressing them by name and exchanging words with them individually every day.

While relationally effective schools will work to develop both teachers' and students' relational acuity, those efforts should be guided by the finding in this and other studies that the teacher must accept the role of relationship manager. Just as the teacher establishes course content, pedagogical method, and behavioral expectations for classes, the teacher is also primarily responsible for initiating relationship, monitoring its progress, and addressing breaches when they occur. It is further understood that teachers will assume these responsibilities in accordance with a school- and community-wide understanding of appropriate boundaries of teacher-student relationships, the aim of which is always to advance students' scholastic mastery and personal growth, never to fill emotional needs of teachers.

The instructive contrast in our study between teachers' narratives of successful and unsuccessful relationships points to a key distinction: in positive accounts, the teacher manages, despite sometimes great resistance, to persist and to reach through to the boy behind the "problem." Responsive to the boy's verbal and behavioral feedback, the teacher draws from a repertoire of relational gestures until the right notes are struck and a learning partnership is initiated. In negative accounts, by contrast, many teachers, preoccupied by their own frustrations or by threats to their self-esteem, fall back to self-management.

Teachers abdicate their role as relationship manager when they are overwhelmed and when their coping resources—both internal and professional—are outmatched by the challenges they face. Andy Hargreaves of Harvard University has carefully studied teacher stress and has detailed what he calls the "emotional politics of teaching," acknowledging that feelings of powerlessness may be especially unbearable for teachers whose identities depend upon being liked or welcomed by their students. When emotionally depleted or confronted with intractable resistance, teachers are vulnerable to "flooding" and may become "extremely defensive, hostile, or withdrawn." Occupational stress and burnout are among the emotional hazards of teaching. In response to feeling overwhelmed, teachers may become hypervigilant in protecting themselves against personal invalidation.[7]

Relationally successful teachers understand that many factors bear upon a boy's ability to participate in trusting and productive relationships. Understanding the influence of these historic and extracurricular factors may generate ideas for reaching a boy, just as successes achieved by prior teachers can suggest strategies that have succeeded in the past. As relationship managers, teachers must also take these other aspects of boys' lives into account:

- The likely reasons for boys' standing resistance to scholastic engagement (i.e., their prior scholastic experiences, domestic circumstances, cultural influences, and prevailing attitudes).
- Boys' relational experience with other colleagues, especially in instances in which the latter may offer suggestions for successful approaches.
- Central extracurricular and out-of-school developments in boys' lives that may shed light on the observed relational stresses and offer alternative opportunities for relationship.

Teachers seeking collegial support in building and maintaining better relationships with students stand to benefit by adopting approaches to professional growth proven to be successful in other specialized occupations. An especially promising strategy is for individual practitioners, however proficient and long-serving in their respective fields, to select a "peer coach" with established expertise with whom to share and observe current practice. Demonstrably effective—and personally stimulating—in fields ranging from surgery to athletics, peer coaches are readily at hand, if not on a teacher's own faculty, not far afield.[8]

THE STUDENT'S ROLE IN RELATIONSHIP

There was no clearer finding in our study than that teachers, not boys, must take responsibility for initiating and then maintaining productive relationship. In the language of the "care initiative," teachers are the *carers* and students are the ones *cared for*. But because oppositional and resistant gestures from boys accounted for a high number of the relational failures reported by teachers, it is important to clarify what teachers contending with especially challenging students can fairly be expected to do.[9]

In addition to the aforementioned relational strategies found to be effective in overcoming a student's standing resistance to classroom engagement—that is, the teacher's refusal to personalize opposition and the willingness to address opposition, typically outside the classroom, in a manner the student perceives as the teacher's attempt to better understand the problem and to help, rather than to correct and punish—it is important, with the aid of colleagues, for a teacher to determine the prior scholastic and personal experience that might have contributed to the resistant posture. More profoundly perhaps, individual teachers and school leaders alike might step back to assess the part that curricular overreliance on cognitive skills—as opposed to essential noncognitive skills such as persistence, self-control, and curiosity—play in students' negative assessments of scholastic challenges and their own likelihood of meeting them. Schools' increasing willingness to reconsider the affective dimensions of their students through such initiatives as the Collaborative for the Advancement of Social and Emotional Learning inform and strengthen the commitment to relational teaching and learning.[10]

Although the relational responsibilities of teacher and student are by no means equal, they are nonetheless mutual. Recognizing and encouraging a boy's capacity for empathic response to both peers and adults is an integral part of his scholastic instruction. To the extent that a student forms his ideas of ethical citizenship from his relational experience, not simply from parents', preachers', and teachers' words, it is important that as he is *cared for* by his teacher he also learns how to be a *receiver of care*, with its own attendant responsibilities. As Nel Noddings has written: "Teachers have special responsibilities that students cannot assume . . . teachers must, that is, take on a dual perspective: their own and that of their students . . . But students have a responsibility too. As recipients of care, they must respond to their teachers' efforts . . . Unless they can respond to caring attempts, they will not grow, and they will certainly not learn to care for others. The responsibilities of teachers and students are necessarily unequal, but they are nonetheless mutual; the relationship is marked by reciprocity."[11]

In addition to modeling empathic response, relationally committed teachers take care in both classroom settings and individual conferences to address relational prerequisites such as engaged listening, withholding critical judgment, and a habit of reflection. The narratives composing our study document the emergent civility and generous regard for others cultivated in boys by teachers who successfully established a relational climate safe for asking for help and admitting frustration and confusion. In such a climate, the beckoning prospect of eventual mastery can overcome what for resistant students had been an inhibiting shame and fear of failure. These growing skills can be the basis for a boy's taking some responsibility for successful engagement with his teachers.

The teacher-student advisory systems in place in many schools too often limit themselves to communicating schoolwide concerns, announcing coming events, and tracking student attendance. But given sufficient commitment to orienting faculty advisors to relational practice, advisory systems could set the relational climate for the school. Advisory clusters are natural settings for reviewing with individual students or with groups the dynamics at play in students' ongoing successful and unsuccessful relationships. Faculty advisors could well serve as relational coaches, mediating when appropriate when either students or teachers register a scholastic or relational concern.

A CONCLUDING PERSPECTIVE

We conducted this study of relationship's place in the scholastic fortunes of boys in response to mounting indications that boys, in the aggregate, are not thriving scholastically. We knew also that, those dire indicators notwithstanding, some boys in some schools—schools of all types—were not only thriving but excelling. More hopeful still: some boys in some schools were transformed from unsuccessful, resistant students to achieving scholars. We wanted to know in what circumstances and in what settings those positive transformations occurred and if that knowledge might be portable to other school settings.

As we have documented in the foregoing, there is indeed a transformative element in relational teaching, and it is both portable and attainable. The capacity to forge and to manage mutually respectful, purposeful relationships with students is developable. While there may certainly be relational "naturals," relational success resides less in inherent gifts than in the extension of specific relational gestures motivated by a commitment that the students in one's charge succeed.

It is emotionally easy—it feels right—to affirm and appreciate the salutary effect of warm teacher-student relationships. What is less easy is to put aside prevailing orthodoxies, such as the dubious assumption that scholastic improvement can be realized through children being coached to score higher on standardized tests. Our findings join a parade of others pointing out that relational teaching and learning is the answer precisely because relationally deficient teaching and learning have created the problem.

The teachers in our study who shared with us their relational successes documented more than the heartening scholastic and behavioral advances of their students. They documented in a thousand distinctive voices that, more than any other factor in their work, struggling and then succeeding in establishing relationship—connecting emotionally—with a boy made a life in teaching worth living.

APPENDIX

—— ■ ■ ■ ——

Research Methods
for the Relational
Teaching Study

IN CHOOSING TO INVESTIGATE relational teaching practices with boys, the research team made several strategic choices for the design of our study at the outset. First, we decided that teachers and boys themselves were the best source of knowledge about what was working and what was not, wishing to situate educational expertise at the teacher and classroom level. To capture this knowledge, we sampled three separate data sources, recognizing the need for triangulation in studying such an interpersonal and multifaceted phenomenon.[1]

We also decided to partner, as in our first study, with the International Boys' Schools Coalition, which agreed to commission the research project in return for a separate report to its membership.[2] The Coalition currently includes two hundred eighty-five single-sex schools, primarily in English-speaking countries. Our experience in the first study had been that though these schools represent a unique school context, their focus exclusively on boys motivates them to scrutinize relational practices that are tacit in school curricula and quite difficult for participants to describe. We found a willing sponsorship of our research from both the Coalition and its member schools.

In basing our study exclusively within single-sex schools for boys, however, we neither endorse the single-sex model nor offer a critique of it. In our experience, what makes a good school for boys is a commitment to their well-being and a willingness to think afresh about cultural assumptions embedded in historic masculinity curricula. We share the view of Marcus Weaver-Hightower that there is "much progressive potential in understanding at a public level that boys, too, have a gender." Political controversy surrounding the single-sex form, especially since the expansion of Title IX allowing public single-sex classrooms and schools in the United States and the parliamentary report encouraging the form in Australia, notwithstanding, at the level of the teacher-student relationship we hoped to discover dynamic practices that worked and ones that did not. Our goal was to elucidate these dynamics and their guiding principles.[3]

Questions of the generalizability of our findings to other school contexts legitimately arise as a result of our exclusively single-sex school sample. Yet in the Teaching Boys study, we found that practices described by teachers and boys in single-sex contexts were immediately recognizable and relevant to teachers in other kinds of schools. From a theoretical perspective, we concluded that gender itself does indeed influence the pedagogy boys elicit from their teachers in reciprocal classroom interactions. School contexts set a broad frame for teacher-student relationships, but within classrooms and in relationships with individual students teachers respond as much to interpersonal and group dynamics. On the basis of the experience from our first study and these observations about teachers' behavior in their relationships with students, we expected broad relevance for relational practices reported from boys' schools classrooms.

The scientific validity of our qualitative approach comes down to its "trustworthiness," and derives from several considerations: accuracy of description and interpretation, theoretical understanding of the subject by the researchers, and, most importantly, the practical

Participating Schools

Australia	Canada	New Zealand	South Africa	United Kingdom	United States
Anglican Church Grammar School	Crescent School	Hamilton Boys' High School	Hilton College	Loughborough Grammar School	The Allen Stevenson School
Christ Church Grammar School	Neil McNeil High School	Lindisfarne College	Maritzburg College	Poole Grammar School	Belmont Hill School
The Scots College	Royal Saint George's College	Palmerston North Boys High School	The Ridge School	Rokeby School	Boys' Latin School of Maryland
Southport School	Selwyn House School		Saint Andrew's College	Saint James Senior Boys' School	The Buckley School
Trinity Grammar School Kew	Upper Canada College		South African College High School	The Windsor Boys' School	Bridgton Academy
				Queen Elizabeth Grammar School (Senior)	Chaminade Catholic High School
					Fenn School
					Gilman School
					Saint Alban's School
					Saint Christopher's School
					Washington Jesuit Academy

usefulness of the study's outcomes. Other commentators have added "authenticity" as key to the validity of qualitative research, a consideration that commits researchers to rigorous and particular research practices, including efforts at triangulation and member checking. Of special importance is "catalytic authenticity": the degree to which the project and its findings "facilitate and stimulate" action.[4]

But we also extended the sample more purposefully in this second study, striving to include schools whose students represented a broader mix of socioeconomic and racial circumstances.[5] Fortunately, the membership of the Coalition includes a cross-section of school types—historic, elite, and fee charging; church-based and parochial; urban and government-funded. For this project a broad invitation was issued to any member school wishing to participate, and our school sample ranged from the most elite U.S. day schools to the recently created Washington Jesuit Academy in the District of Columbia; from 100 percent state-supported, urban schools like Neil McNeil High School in Toronto or Rokeby School in London to the Saint John's Northwestern Military Academy in the woods of Wisconsin. To ensure that the sample included a diversity of school types, schools from government-funded, urban contexts were more actively solicited.

Overall, thirty-six schools from six English-speaking participated in the study.

The participating schools, as this list attests, ranged from historic, elite boys' schools to government-funded, comprehensive high schools to relatively new inner-city schools restricted to small numbers of minority boys. Across the different school contexts we looked for common themes in the types of relationship experiences reported by boys and teachers.

Once the school sample was finalized, we began collecting data, sampling three separate data sources.

ONLINE SURVEY

First, we conducted online surveys of teachers and students. For the teacher survey, schools were instructed to invite all faculty members working with middle and upper school boys to participate. Prior to beginning, the project coordinator at each school explained the project and its aims. Teachers were invited to complete the online survey on their own, at their own pace, over a several-week period.

After a short introduction and several demographic questions, the survey consisted of two main tasks.

- **Task 1:** Describe a relationship with a boy that resulted in especially gratifying achievement or improvement. The achievement/improvement could be in either his scholastic performance or his behavior.
- **Task 2:** Describe a relationship with a student you felt you were not able to reach effectively. The boy in question could be one who you feel did not satisfactorily engage in the subject you were teaching or whose classroom behavior was unresponsive to your efforts to instruct him.

Of the nearly twelve hundred teachers who completed the survey, 35 percent were from the United States; 16 percent came from South Africa; 16 percent came from New Zealand; 15 percent were from Canada; 13 percent were from Australia; and 5 percent were from the United Kingdom. Male teachers outnumbered female by two to one, and overall, teachers ranged evenly from one year's to forty years' experience teaching.

In addition to the teacher survey, the project also surveyed a sample of students from each participating school, asking parallel questions. For the student survey, schools were instructed to collect a sample of middle and upper school students and arrange for them to respond to our brief online questionnaire during school hours. Schools handled this task differently, some sampling single classes of perhaps thirty students while others sampled their entire upper school. The survey coordinator at each school explained the project to the students and invited those who were willing to participate. It was understood by the students that only research team members would see their responses and that their confidentiality would be protected throughout the research and reporting process.

The student survey also consisted of two tasks.

- **Task 1:** Describe a positive relationship you have had with a teacher. It could be a teacher who inspired you to explore material and ideas you otherwise would not have explored. It may have been a teacher who helped you understand material you felt you were not interested in or able to master. It may have been a teacher whose manner somehow inspired you to do your best work.
- **Task 2:** Describe a relationship with a teacher that did not work for you, one in which the teacher's manner or approach to the material made it hard for you to maintain interest and to do your best.

In the student sample, 38 percent of respondents attended school in the United Kingdom; 27 percent in the United States; 12 percent in Canada; 9 percent in South Africa; 8 percent in Australia; and 6 percent in New Zealand.

In addition to their country of origin, student respondents described their motivation and achievement levels, as well as their racial and socioeconomic positions. In the sample, 78 percent described themselves as either highly or well motivated; 17 percent described their motivation as average; 5 percent described themselves as somewhat less motivated; and only 1 percent said they were not motivated at all.

In terms of academic achievement, 25 percent of student respondents described themselves as at the top; 49 percent said they were above average; 23 percent were average; and only 2 percent placed themselves below average.

Economically, 13 percent of respondents described their families as in the top socioeconomic category; 48 percent said they were above average; 33 percent said they were average; and 6 percent—a total of seventy-three students—said they came from below average circumstances. Racially, 59 percent of respondents described themselves as members of the majority ethnic group; 25 percent from a minority; and 16 percent said that their ethnic status was uncertain.

In analyzing the survey data, the research team engaged in an iterative coding process with an initial set of themes deduced separately by each of three researchers and the second set representing a synthesis worked out during daylong coding sessions.[6] Interteam differences fostered clarifying and challenging discussions that facilitated the new coding framework, which then served as a basis for the next two research phases.

In these phases the researchers' initial themes and interpretations were explored in follow-up focus groups and workshops with teachers and students. This member check process provided detailed feedback, helping us to refine our conclusions.[7]

FOCUS GROUP INTERVIEWS

Given its focus on students' and teachers' personal reactions and interpretations in relationships, we needed to ensure that our understanding of survey responses accurately reflected what respondents meant. Therefore, we also conducted a series of focus groups with both boys and teachers. We met with several focus groups of both students and teachers at Maritzburg College in Pietermaritzburg, South Africa; at Saint James Senior Boys' School in Ashford, England; at both Upper Canada College and Neil McNeil High School in Toronto, Canada; and at Boys' Latin School of Baltimore in the United States. Students and teachers were selected for interviews by the school coordinator based upon our suggestions: to include male as well as female teachers, new as well as veteran teachers, students who represented both dominant and minority racial groups, and students who were successful as well as those less successful.

To analyze data collected from these sources, the research team used two approaches: (1) grounded theory, and (2) thematic analysis. Within these approaches, the research team used "open coding" to "break down, examine, compare, conceptualize, and categorize" the focus group data into coherent themes.[8] Each member of the research team was initially responsible for coding several interviews and for contrasting emergent themes with the existing framework from survey analyses. Discussions between team members facilitated the refinement of the thematic framework.

RELATIONAL TEACHING WORKSHOPS

Unique to the research design of this project, the Relational Teaching workshop was intended to provide the research team with a better understanding—specifically exploring approaches to helping teachers improve skills in this area—achievable only in "live" interaction with school people committed to mutual discovery and explication. The workshop was composed of teachers and senior staff who were designated by their respective school administrators as relational teaching leaders. They were also chosen because they were committed to the project's goals and would agree to serve as a testing ground for themes and recommendations emerging from survey responses. The research team conducted these daylong workshops in the United States, South Africa, and the United Kingdom, with groups varying from twenty-five to seventy-five participants. At the workshops in South Africa and England, we included a panel of students so that teachers would have an opportunity to respond to boys and discuss issues with them.

The stated goals of the workshops were:

- To offer a live "member check" for survey interpretation; for the research team to present emerging themes for additional insight and interpretative feedback, ensuring that each country's schools participated in shaping outcomes.
- To provide an opportunity to deepen and explore teachers' reflections about relational teaching, with the goal of developing a viable school-based model for ongoing professional growth in relational pedagogy.
- To offer an experience of professional development for participants as they tested emerging models for professional development in relational learning.
- To help mobilizing teams from each participating school to support the work of relational teaching. It was hoped that